JESUS

HIS LIFE

JESUS

HIS LIFE

A COMPANION GUIDE

FaithWords HISTORY
New York • Nashville

FaithWords
Hachette Book Group
1290 Avenue of the Americas, New York, NY 10104

www.faithwords.com
twitter.com/faithwords

First Edition: March 2019

FaithWords is a division of Hachette Book Group, Inc. The FaithWords name and logo are trademarks of Hachette Book Group, Inc.

The publisher is not responsible for websites (or their content) that are not owned by the publisher.

Published with the assistance of Hudson Bible.
Cover design by Matt Smartt, Smartt Guys Design.
Front cover and interior photos by José Sarmento Matos.
Print book interior design by Bart Dawson.

Cataloging-in-Publication Data is on file with the Library of Congress.

ISBN: 978-1-54603-853-5 (trade paper)

Printed in the United States of America
LSC-C
10 9 8 7 6 5 4 3 2 1

CONTENTS

FOREWORD
by Joel Osteen

For more than 2,000 years and to billions of people around the world, Jesus is the most important person who has ever lived. To those who believe, He is the Son of God, the Messiah, and the Savior of all mankind. To those who don't, He is still considered one of, if not the most, significant figure in human history. His life and teachings have influenced societies and governments across the globe, and His legacy endures as one of love and compassion.

How could a ministry lasting only three years have such an undeniable impact on the entire world? The answer to this question has been contemplated by theologians, philosophers, and academics for more than two millennia, and it's one that affects the lives of billions of ordinary people to this day.

In many ways our present is the product of our history. To understand our modern world we must first understand the ancient one that preceded it and those who shaped it. If we look closely, we can see in these ancient people many of the same choices we make today. We experience the same joys, fear, anger, sadness, and love that they felt; and we exhibit the same courage, ambition, forgiveness, and loyalty that became the hallmark of a life well lived or not so well lived. But, above all, we experience and express a faith that was born in those days of upheaval; a faith that endures in believers today.

This book is a companion guide to HISTORY's eight-part series on the life of Jesus as told through the eyes of those who witnessed His words and deeds. Some were family, friends, and followers, while others opposed Him. Regardless of their relationship to Him, their lives were profoundly affected by Him. Each of their stories provides a unique insight into the man billions consider to be God himself.

As you watch the television series and journey through this guide, I encourage you to carefully examine not only Jesus and His life but the actions of each person affected by Him. Place yourself in their shoes, imagine facing the choices they faced, and think about how you would respond. You will see how each individual played an exceptional and necessary role in this monumental story and you will not only gain a clearer understanding of Jesus, His mission, and the times during which He lived, but you will undoubtedly learn something about yourself, as well.

EPISODE 1

JOSEPH

Lesson 1: Anticipation

Lesson 2: Trust

Lesson 3: Protection

Lesson 1
ANTICIPATION

Joseph wanted to work,
raise a family, and build a house
in Nazareth for the woman he loved.
— Jesus: His Life

Joseph was excited. He was nervous too, but mostly excited. It had been three months since Mary had left. Three months of preparation, three months of planning, three months of anticipation.

They would build a life together. They would have a house, a garden, and—if God was merciful—children. They would do what God commanded the first man and the first woman to do so long ago: be fruitful and multiply.

For a man of his position, it was everything he could want. Unless the Messiah arrived and brought in God's Kingdom, he and Mary would build a life and a family in Nazareth. They wouldn't be rich, but they would have each other.

It would be a good life.

OPENING QUESTION

1. What is the biggest event or experience you've ever anticipated? Why were you so excited about it?

READING THE STORY

Luke 1:26–33 (ESV)

In the sixth month the angel Gabriel was sent from God to a city of Galilee named Nazareth, to a virgin betrothed to a man whose name was Joseph, of the house of David. And the virgin's name was Mary. And he came to her and said, "Greetings, O favored one, the Lord is with you!" But she was greatly troubled at the saying, and tried to discern what sort of greeting this might be. And the angel said to her, "Do not be afraid, Mary, for you have found favor with God. And behold, you will conceive in your womb and bear a son, and you shall call his name Jesus. He will be great and will be called the Son of the Most High. And the Lord God will give to him the throne of his father David, and he will reign over the house of Jacob forever, and of his kingdom there will be no end."

Luke 1:36–40 (ESV)

And behold, your relative Elizabeth in her old age has also conceived a son, and this is the sixth month with her who was called barren. For nothing will be impossible with God." And Mary said, "Behold, I am the servant of the Lord; let it be to me according to your word." And the angel departed from her. In those days Mary arose and went with haste into the hill country, to a town in Judah, and she entered the house of Zechariah and greeted Elizabeth.

ENGAGING THE STORY

2. Why do you think Mary went to see Elizabeth instead of telling Joseph about her visit from the angel?

3. If you had been Joseph, how might you have felt about Mary leaving for 3 months just before you were to be married?

4. What kind of thoughts do you think Mary might have had about Joseph as she traveled home from Elizabeth's house?

"One reason that Joseph is important to me is that God chose a common man to do something uncommon."

— Joel Osteen (Jesus: His Life)

EXPLORING THE THEMES

Luke 2:25–32 (NIV)

Now there was a man in Jerusalem called Simeon, who was righteous and devout. He was waiting for the consolation of Israel, and the Holy Spirit was on him. It had been revealed to him by the Holy Spirit that he would not die before he had seen the Lord's Messiah. Moved by the Spirit, he went into the temple courts. When the parents brought in the child Jesus to do for him what the custom of the Law required, Simeon took him in his arms and praised God, saying: "Sovereign Lord, as you have promised, you may now dismiss your servant in peace. For my eyes have seen your salvation, which you have prepared in the sight of all nations: a light for revelation to the Gentiles, and the glory of your people Israel."

Many people had been anticipating the coming of the Messiah. Jesus was the fulfillment of a promise made thousands of years earlier. The Jewish prophets had foretold His coming and the Jewish people had prayed for it.

While Jesus' birth went unnoticed by most people in Israel, there was one man who had been eagerly anticipating the Messiah. God had actually promised Simeon that he would not die before he saw the Messiah.

Luke's mention of Simeon reminds us of a key component of God's character: He keeps His promises. God kept His promises to Israel about sending the Messiah. God kept His promise to Simeon that he wouldn't die before he saw the Messiah. Thus we can be sure God will keep His promises to us.

5. If you had been Joseph, how might you feel about being the father (actually the legal guardian) of the Messiah?

6. If you had been Simeon, how do you think you would have felt as you woke up every morning anticipating the coming of the Messiah? How might you have felt when you went to bed each night without seeing Him?

7. How do you think Simeon felt as he finally held Jesus in his arms?

"For my eyes have seen your salvation, which you have prepared in the sight of all nations . . ."

— Luke 2:30–31 (NIV)

EXPERIENCING THE STORY

Think about your life. What are you anticipating? What is the basis for your anticipation? What would you like to see God do in the next season of your life?

Lesson 2

TRUST

How could any man accept Mary's story?
How could Joseph possibly believe she was carrying
the Son of God? . . . But what if Mary's story was true?
—Jesus: His Life

She had betrayed him, but that wasn't what hurt the most. Betrayal he could overcome, but the story. . . . Did she think he was a fool? An angel? Really? It wasn't enough that she threw away their future together for someone else; she had to concoct a ridiculous story on top of it.

Didn't she know what he could do to her? If he wanted to, he could destroy her life. One public accusation, and she would be forever tainted in Nazareth. Some of the older members of the town might even suggest stoning her.

Even as he thought about it, he knew that wasn't what he would choose. She had hurt him, yes, but she didn't deserve to be publicly disgraced. He still loved her, even though she had broken his heart.

What if her story was true? No. It couldn't be.

Unless God Himself said otherwise, Joseph would end their engagement.

OPENING QUESTION

1. What's the biggest surprise you've ever experienced? What happened?

READING THE STORY

Matthew 1:18–25 (NIV)

This is how the birth of Jesus the Messiah came about: His mother Mary was pledged to be married to Joseph, but before they came together, she was found to be pregnant through the Holy Spirit. Because Joseph her husband was faithful to the law, and yet did not want to expose her to public disgrace, he had in mind to divorce her quietly.

But after he had considered this, an angel of the Lord appeared to him in a dream and said, "Joseph son of David, do not be afraid to take Mary home as your wife, because what is conceived in her is from the Holy Spirit. She will give birth to a son, and you are to give him the name Jesus, because he will save his people from their sins."

All this took place to fulfill what the Lord had said through the prophet: "The virgin will conceive and give birth to a son, and they will call him Immanuel" (which means "God with us").

When Joseph woke up, he did what the angel of the Lord had commanded him and took Mary home as his wife. But he did not consummate their marriage until she gave birth to a son. And he gave him the name Jesus.

ENGAGING THE STORY

2. Why do you think Joseph decided to send Mary away quietly instead of publicly disgracing her? What do you think that decision says about Joseph's character?

3. What do you think everyone in Nazareth thought of Mary and Joseph when they found out she was pregnant? How do you think Joseph felt about the talk throughout his village?

4. Why do you think God chose to speak to Joseph through a dream? If you had been Joseph, how might you have responded to the dream?

"The virgin will conceive and give birth to a son, and they will call him Immanuel" (which means "God with us").

— Matthew 1:23 (NIV)

EXPLORING THE THEMES

Luke 2:22–24 (NIV)

When the time came for the purification rites required by the Law of Moses, Joseph and Mary took him to Jerusalem to present him to the Lord (as it is written in the Law of the Lord, "Every firstborn male is to be consecrated to the Lord"), and to offer a sacrifice in keeping with what is said in the Law of the Lord: "a pair of doves or two young pigeons."

Luke 2:33, 36–39 (NIV)

The child's father and mother marveled at what was said about him. . . . There was also a prophet, Anna, the daughter of Penuel, of the tribe of Asher. She was very old; she had lived with her husband seven years after her marriage, and then was a widow until she was eighty-four. She never left the temple but worshiped night and day, fasting and praying. Coming up to them at that very moment, she gave thanks to God and spoke about the child to all who were looking forward to the redemption of Jerusalem.

When Joseph and Mary had done everything required by the Law of the Lord, they returned to Galilee to their own town of Nazareth.

We can easily fall apart when our world caves in, whether from losing a loved one or a job, dealing with a health crisis or a financial disaster, or suffering from deep depression. Sometimes it's hard to get up in the morning and put one foot in front of the other.

Joseph probably felt this way when he learned about Mary's unplanned pregnancy. His world turned upside down in a moment! Even so, he continued to exercise trust in God by doing what God had said specifically (through a dream) and what He had said generally (through the law).

No matter what happens in our lives, we can trust in the God who is faithful and has proven Himself trustworthy. Throughout the Bible we see He is a loving, kind, gracious, merciful God. The more we learn to trust Him, the more we experience the blessings of being in relationship with Him. If we surrender our lives to Him and trust Him for everything, He will guide us and walk with us step by step through anything that comes our way.

5. What did Joseph do in Jerusalem that demonstrated his trust in God? How do we demonstrate our trust in God today?

6. If you had been Anna, how easy would it have been for you to continue trusting God as a widow for many decades? What did her words and actions in the presence of Joseph's family suggest about her trust in God?

7. Do you think it was ever difficult for Joseph, Mary, and Anna to trust God to keep His promises? How have you experienced similar struggles in your life?

EXPERIENCING THE STORY

How has God been faithful to you in the past? When did you struggle to trust God? What did it take for you to trust Him again?

Lesson 3

PROTECTION

Every new father thinks his child is special,
that things will never be the same again.
But when Jesus came into Joseph's life, He changed it forever.
— Jesus: His Life

This wasn't how Joseph expected his life to turn out. When he first held Jesus in his arms that night in Bethlehem, Joseph knew that his child was special. But he couldn't have imagined how special Jesus was—shepherds don't show up to worship normal children.

Normal children don't have kings from faraway lands bring them gifts either. They had looked at his son and given Him gifts—more extravagant gifts than Joseph had ever seen! He was just a carpenter from Nazareth, and now he had been thrust into a world of angels, kings, and dreams.

The dreams. He kept having them. It was why they had left Bethlehem. Mary had trusted him. The gifts the wise men brought them had given them the funds they needed to settle in Egypt. From what they heard on their travels, they had left just in time.

Was this going to be his life—constantly fleeing from those who were threatened by his child and wanted to harm Him? If that was the case, so be it. God had protected them this far.

God would continue to protect them.

OPENING QUESTION

1. Do you think dreams allow us to process things going on in real life? Has a dream ever impacted you for several days?

READING THE STORY

Matthew 2:13–15 (NIV)

When they had gone, an angel of the Lord appeared to Joseph in a dream. "Get up," he said, "take the child and his mother and escape to Egypt. Stay there until I tell you, for Herod is going to search for the child to kill him." So he got up, took the child and his mother during the night and left for Egypt, where he stayed until the death of Herod. And so was fulfilled what the Lord had said through the prophet: "Out of Egypt I called my son."

ENGAGING THE STORY

2. How do you think Joseph felt when he realized that shepherds, foreign travelers, and King Herod were all interested in his child?

3. Why do you think God continued speaking to Joseph in dreams? If you had been Mary, how might you have responded when Joseph told you about the dreams he was having?

4. How might Joseph have struggled with the fact that Jesus wasn't his biological son?

Joseph had to protect his son from dangers no normal father would ever face.

— Jesus: His Life

EXPLORING THE THEMES

Matthew 2:9–12 (NIV)

After they had heard the king, they went on their way, and the star they had seen when it rose went ahead of them until it stopped over the place where the child was. When they saw the star, they were overjoyed. On coming to the house, they saw the child with his mother Mary, and they bowed down and worshiped him. Then they opened their treasures and presented him with gifts of gold, frankincense and myrrh. And having been warned in a dream not to go back to Herod, they returned to their country by another route.

Matthew 2:16–18 (NIV)

When Herod realized that he had been outwitted by the Magi, he was furious, and he gave orders to kill all the boys in Bethlehem and its vicinity who were two years old and under, in accordance with the time he had learned from the Magi. Then what was said through the prophet Jeremiah was fulfilled: "A voice is heard in Ramah, weeping and great mourning, Rachel weeping for her children and refusing to be comforted, because they are no more."

The moment Jesus was born, Joseph was thrust into a role far beyond that of a normal father. Beyond caring for this infant's health and well-being, Joseph had to protect Jesus from complicated diplomatic threats. Suddenly, the simple carpenter from Nazareth was entertaining foreign kings and fleeing from a disturbed ruler who wanted to kill his child. How was one man—Joseph—supposed to stand against the might of King Herod?

The truth was that Joseph didn't face those events alone. God protected Joseph, Mary, and Jesus. As His followers, God promises to protect us as well!

5. Why do you think God chose to protect Joseph, Mary, and Jesus by having them flee to Egypt?

6. If you had been Joseph, how might you have felt when you heard that all the young boys in Bethlehem had been murdered?

7. What are some ways God might have protected us and kept us from harm without us realizing it?

"So he got up, took the child and his mother during the night and left for Egypt, where he stayed until the death of Herod. And so was fulfilled what the Lord had said through the prophet: 'Out of Egypt I called my son.'"

— Matthew 2:14–15 (NIV)

EXPERIENCING THE STORY

Think about your story. When has God protected you? How did He do it? How did His protection change your relationship with Him?

EPISODE 2

JOHN THE BAPTIST

Lesson 1: Replacement

Lesson 2: Revelation

Lesson 3: Defeat

Lesson 1

REPLACEMENT

John was put on earth to do one thing.
One divine purpose.
— Jesus: His Life

For centuries, the people of Israel had been waiting for a Messiah whose coming had been foretold by the prophets, God's spokesmen. The Messiah would come to save His people from their sins. The prophet Malachi, who wrote the very last book of the Old Testament, promised one who would come before the Messiah. That person would be a prophet like Elijah, the greatest prophet in Israel's history. However, after Malachi finished writing, there were no more prophets. It was like God was silent for 400 years.

Finally, John the Baptist broke the silence. He was the son of a priest but didn't follow in his father's footsteps. Instead, John lived in the wilderness of Judea, where he preached a fiery message of repentance that would prepare Israel for their Messiah.

As Malachi had foretold, a prophet like Elijah had come.

John gathered a following and developed a reputation. He had disciples who hung on his every word, he baptized those who embraced his message, and he confronted the brokenness and corruption he saw in society. He was a man on the rise—a popular preacher sought out by many. However, John knew his ministry wasn't about him. The crowds, popularity, and controversy weren't intended to make him famous. Instead, they were tools for him to use to accomplish his purpose: preparing Israel for the Light that God had sent into a dark world, a light that would soon outshine, overshadow, and eclipse his own.

OPENING QUESTION

1. Have you ever had to train someone you knew would replace you in your position? How did you handle that experience? If you've never had that experience, how do you think you might handle it?

READING THE STORY

Matthew 3:1–8, 11–12 (ESV)

In those days John the Baptist came preaching in the wilderness of Judea, "Repent, for the kingdom of heaven is at hand." For this is he who was spoken of by the prophet Isaiah when he said,

"The voice of one crying in the wilderness: 'Prepare the way of the Lord; make his paths straight.'"

Now John wore a garment of camel's hair and a leather belt around his waist, and his food was locusts and wild honey. Then Jerusalem and all Judea and all the region about the Jordan were going out to him, and they were baptized by him in the river Jordan, confessing their sins.

But when he saw many of the Pharisees and Sadducees coming to his baptism, he said to them, "You brood of vipers! Who warned you to flee from the wrath to come? Bear fruit in keeping with repentance. . . .

"I baptize you with water for repentance, but he who is coming after me is mightier than I, whose sandals I am not worthy to carry. He will baptize you with the Holy Spirit and fire. His winnowing fork is in his hand, and he will clear his threshing floor and gather his wheat into the barn, but the chaff he will burn with unquenchable fire."

ENGAGING THE STORY

2. John urged people to repent. What does it mean to repent? Why do you suppose that was such an important message in John's ministry?

3. John indicated his role was to fade into the background, so that everyone could focus on Jesus. If you had been in John's shoes, would it be easy or hard for you to accept this diminishing role? Why?

4. Why do you think John felt unworthy to carry Jesus' sandals?

EXPLORING THE THEMES

John 3:27–30 (ESV)

John answered, "A person cannot receive even one thing unless it is given him from heaven. You yourselves bear me witness, that I said, 'I am not the Christ, but I have been sent before him.' The one who has the bride is the bridegroom. The friend of the bridegroom, who stands and hears him, rejoices greatly at the bridegroom's voice. Therefore this joy of mine is now complete. He must increase, but I must decrease."

On any social media platform, you'll see dozens of messages all with the same theme: "Me, me, me, me." Had Twitter been invented in the days of John the Baptist, his tweets would be short and sweet: *It's not about ME; it's all about HIM. #Repent*

John had a successful ministry but he knew he was merely a cheerleader for someone else. He lived in the certainty of that calling. John knew his life was all about one thing—preparing to meet Jesus. John wasn't just okay with Jesus overshadowing and eclipsing him; John knew that was God's plan and purpose. Just like John the Baptist, not only are we called to tell people about Jesus, but we're also called to let Jesus overshadow us—to let Him (not us) be the one people see and follow.

> *John had always thought the Messiah would bring a wave of destruction. The Messiah wouldn't come to John for answers. He* is *the answer.*
>
> — Jesus: His Life

5. What are some of the ways people struggle with the role their faith plays in their life at times?

6. Is there anyone in your life who needs to experience the Light that has come into the world? How can you be like John and prepare the way for them to encounter Jesus?

7. Why do you think John felt joy as Jesus overshadowed and eclipsed him? Have you ever experienced joy when someone surpassed you? Why or why not?

EXPERIENCING THE STORY

Where in your life (job, family, hobbies, church) have you made your life about you? What would it look like for you to make your life about telling people that Light (Jesus) has come into the world?

Lesson 2

REVELATION

John should have seen, there was more to Jesus than John knew.

— Jesus: His Life

John was waiting. He had left Jerusalem, the Temple, and his family to go into the wilderness. As the crowds followed him, he told them what he knew. The time their ancestors had anticipated had almost arrived. The Messiah's arrival was imminent! The crowds responded. They turned from their old ways of thinking and prepared themselves for the Messiah's appearance. As a symbol of their repentance, John baptized them in the Jordan River.

The Messiah was so close. John could almost feel Him. When He arrived, the words of the prophets from so long ago would come true. The Messiah would come with fire, bringing God's justice upon His enemies. He would rescue His people from oppression and bondage! It would be a pivotal moment. It would be the fulfillment of John's purpose, the culmination of his mission.

Then Jesus arrived. Jesus was John's cousin, just a few months younger than him. Jesus was the carpenter's son, quiet and humble, but confident—already gathering a following of disciples who hung on His every word. Could He really be the Messiah—the one God had promised through the prophets so long ago?

If Jesus was the Messiah, why did He want John to baptize Him?

OPENING QUESTION

1. What's the most extraordinary story someone ever told you about themselves? How easy was it for you to believe them? Why?

READING THE STORY

Matthew 3:13–17 (NKJV)

Then Jesus came from Galilee to John at the Jordan to be baptized by him. And John tried to prevent Him, saying, "I need to be baptized by You, and are You coming to me?"

But Jesus answered and said to him, "Permit it to be so now, for thus it is fitting for us to fulfill all righteousness." Then he allowed Him.

When He had been baptized, Jesus came up immediately from the water; and behold, the heavens were opened to Him, and He saw the Spirit of God descending like a dove and alighting upon Him. And suddenly a voice came from heaven, saying, "This is My beloved Son, in whom I am well pleased."

ENGAGING THE STORY

2. How do you think John viewed Jesus before His baptism? How do you think John's perspective changed after Jesus' baptism?

3. Why do you think God waited until after the baptism to acknowledge that Jesus was His Son?

4. Why do you think Jesus wanted to be baptized by John? If you had been John, how might you have felt as you were baptizing Jesus?

"When He had been baptized, Jesus came up immediately from the water; and behold, the heavens were opened to Him, and He saw the Spirit of God descending like a dove and alighting upon Him."

— Matthew 3:16 (NKJV)

EXPLORING THE THEMES

Matthew 3:17 (NKJV)

And suddenly a voice came from heaven, saying, "This is My beloved Son, in whom I am well pleased."

Matthew 4:16–17 (ESV)

The people dwelling in darkness have seen a great light, and for those dwelling in the region and shadow of death, on them a light has dawned. From that time Jesus began to preach, saying, "Repent, for the kingdom of heaven is at hand."

Jesus' baptism was the beginning of Jesus's public ministry. When God spoke to Jesus in the River Jordan, it revealed to everyone watching that Jesus was more than a man—He was the Son of God. John's entire life had led up to that moment. His mission was to prepare the way for Jesus, to get the people of Israel ready for the Messiah. As Jesus came up out of the water, John saw the fulfillment of his life's mission. The Messiah had come!

We all have moments where God reveals Himself to us. Many times this happens through His Word, other times it's through the words of His people, and sometimes it's through the still, small voice of His Spirit speaking directly to our hearts. No matter how God speaks, when He reveals truth to us, it should also be a turning point in our lives.

John knew by then Jesus was no simple carpenter.

— Jesus: His Life

5. When God spoke, He revealed to John the truth about Jesus. How has God spoken and revealed His truth to you?

6. John's mission was to prepare the way for Jesus. What does it look like for us to prepare the way for Jesus today?

7. Why do you think some people do not believe that Jesus is God's Son?

EXPERIENCING THE STORY

Where do you need God to show you His truth? How would that truth change the way you think and act? How could God's revelation to you have an impact in someone else's life?

Lesson 3
DEFEAT

Was John wrong?
— Jesus: His Life

This wasn't how John thought it would end. Yes, the Messiah had arrived, but the bigger transformation hadn't. Corrupt leaders were still in power. John had tried to make them see the truth—their failure to keep God's commands—and it had landed him in prison.

John's popularity had waned too. Gone were the crowds who used to hang on his every word, who made it impossible for the king and priests to stop him. Some even left to follow Jesus. But where was the revolution? Where was the judgment, the rescue the Messiah was supposed to bring? If Jesus really was the Messiah, why didn't He rescue John from prison? Wasn't the Messiah supposed to set the captives free?

What if John had been wrong? If the Messiah hadn't come, then John's life had been wasted. If Jesus wasn't the One, then John had failed, and Herod and the other corrupt leaders had won. There was only one way to find out, only one way to know whether his life's work had made any difference.

Surely Jesus would answer his question.

OPENING QUESTION

1. Describe a time you tried out for a team or club and didn't make it, or when you interviewed for a job but didn't get it. How did you feel? How did you handle those emotions?

READING THE STORY

Matthew 11:2–6 (NIV)

When John, who was in prison, heard about the deeds of the Messiah, he sent his disciples to ask him, "Are you the one who is to come, or should we expect someone else?"

Jesus replied, "Go back and report to John what you hear and see: The blind receive sight, the lame walk, those who have leprosy are cleansed, the deaf hear, the dead are raised, and the good news is proclaimed to the poor. Blessed is anyone who does not stumble on account of me."

ENGAGING THE STORY

2. Of the questions John could have asked when he was in prison, why do you think he chose to ask Jesus if He was "the one who is to come"? Why do you think Jesus answered as He did?

3. Why do you think Jesus didn't rebuke John for his question? What does this suggest about the types of questions we can take to the Lord?

4. If you had been John, how might you have felt being neglected in prison while crowds of people flocked to Jesus?

Did John do enough?

— Jesus: His Life

EXPLORING THE THEMES

Matthew 14:3–9 (ESV)

Herod had seized John and bound him and put him in prison for the sake of Herodias, his brother Philip's wife, because John had been saying to him, "It is not lawful for you to have her." And though he wanted to put him to death, he feared the people, because they held him to be a prophet. But when Herod's birthday came, the daughter of Herodias danced before the company and pleased Herod, so that he promised with an oath to give her whatever she might ask. Prompted by her mother, she said, "Give me the head of John the Baptist here on a platter." And the king was sorry, but because of his oaths and his guests he commanded it to be given.

Matthew 11:11, 14 (NKJV)

Assuredly, I say to you, among those born of women there has not risen one greater than John the Baptist; but he who is least in the kingdom of heaven is greater than he. . . . And if you are willing to receive it, he is Elijah who is to come.

From external appearances, it looked like John had failed. The crowds were gone. His disciples had left him to follow Jesus. Herod had locked him up in a dungeon. It certainly wasn't the way John thought his ministry would end. Even so, John hadn't been defeated. The Messiah he had devoted his life to proclaiming was here, healing the sick and casting out demons, just like the prophets had foretold. What looked like defeat was really victory!

What was easy to say, however, was harder to believe. That's why John sent messengers to Jesus to ask if He really was the Messiah. John needed assurance that all he had done hadn't been for nothing. We all have moments like this in our lives. In these moments we feel like failures, like we've been defeated, because life didn't live up to our expectations. The good news is Jesus does for us exactly what He did for John the Baptist. Jesus reminds us of His activity—that He's in control and will ultimately be victorious.

5. Being imprisoned was John's low point. How does Jesus' words about John change the way we should view ourselves during similar difficult circumstances?

6. Why do you think God allows us to go through seasons of defeat and disappointment instead of rescuing us immediately?

7. What kinds of experiences might some people consider failures, yet God looks at them as victories?

EXPERIENCING THE STORY

Where in your life do you feel defeated, like you're failing? What do you think God wants to say about you and that part of your life? How might God's truth change the way you think about yourself and what you perceive to be failure?

EPISODE 3

MARY, MOTHER OF JESUS

Lesson 1: Surrender

Lesson 2: Purpose

Lesson 3: Faith

Lesson 1

SURRENDER

Jesus was given to Mary by God to love and nurture.

— Jesus: His Life

No matter what anyone said, He was still her son. Since before He was born, rumors had swirled. She knew what it must have looked like, and no one would believe what happened. An angel? Really? It was miraculous that Joseph hadn't ended their engagement, but it was probably too much to expect that everyone else in Nazareth would gloss over the fact that she was pregnant before they were married.

It went deeper than that, however. Yes, the angel told her He was given to her by God. Yes, she knew He had a divine purpose. Yes, she knew He was the Messiah for whom her people had waited and prayed for centuries. Yet, he was still *her* son. He had lived inside her body for months, and then entered the world on a silent night in a stable in Bethlehem.

It all seemed so long ago. She had watched Him grow up and had taught Him to love God with all His heart, soul, mind, and strength. She had wept when they lost Him in Jerusalem and wept even more when they found Him. Now He was leaving. It was time for Him to fulfill the calling God had given Him before He was even born.

But He would always be her son.

OPENING QUESTION

1. If you were going on vacation, would you rather plan the entire trip yourself and know what would happen every day, or let someone else plan it and be surprised? Why?

READING THE STORY

Luke 1:26–35, 38 (ESV)

In the sixth month the angel Gabriel was sent from God to a city of Galilee named Nazareth, to a virgin betrothed to a man whose name was Joseph, of the house of David. And the virgin's name was Mary. And he came to her and said, "Greetings, O favored one, the Lord is with you!" But she was greatly troubled at the saying, and tried to discern what sort of greeting this might be. And the angel said to her, "Do not be afraid, Mary, for you have found favor with God. And behold, you will conceive in your womb and bear a son, and you shall call his name Jesus. He will be great and will be called the Son of the Most High. And the Lord God will give to him the throne of his father David, and he will reign over the house of Jacob forever, and of his kingdom there will be no end." And Mary said to the angel, "How will this be, since I am a virgin?" And the angel answered her, "The Holy Spirit will come upon you, and the power of the Most High will overshadow you; therefore the child to be born will be called holy—the Son of God. . . . And Mary said, "Behold, I am the servant of the Lord; let it be to me according to your word." And the angel departed from her.

ENGAGING THE STORY

2. If you had been Mary, how might you have responded to the angel's presence? Why?

3. How do you think Mary felt when the angel told her she was going to have a child? What would that announcement have meant for her socially? What about spiritually?

4. What do you think it was like for Mary to be the mother of Jesus? What kinds of struggles and joys do you think she experienced as Jesus' mother?

Mary sensed He would have a divine purpose.

— Jesus: His Life

EXPLORING THE THEMES

Luke 1:43–45 (NKJV)

But why is this granted to me, that the mother of my Lord should come to me? For indeed, as soon as the voice of your greeting sounded in my ears, the babe leaped in my womb for joy. Blessed is she who believed, for there will be a fulfillment of those things which were told her from the Lord."

Luke 1:46–49 (ESV)

And Mary said, "My soul magnifies the Lord, and my spirit rejoices in God my Savior, for he has looked on the humble estate of his servant. For behold, from now on all generations will call me blessed; for he who is mighty has done great things for me, and holy is his name.

Gabriel's announcement changed Mary's life. Of all the women in the world, God chose her to be the human mother of His Son. That decision would make generations of Jesus' followers call her blessed but would also guarantee pain and heartache. Mary knew from before Jesus was born that He was not hers to control. Yet, she still carried Him in her womb, birthed Him, raised Him, and loved Him deeply as her son.

Mary's entire life was one of surrender. Her plans, her reputation, and her life were for God to use as He wished. As followers of Jesus, we're called to be just like Mary: our lives should be fully surrendered to God to build His kingdom as He desires.

5. Why do you think Mary didn't respond in anger or doubt when God altered the course of her life? What does that indicate about how she viewed God?

6. How do you think Mary's surrender to God's plan brought her joy? How do you think it brought her pain?

7. What does it look like for us to surrender our lives to God?

"And Mary said, 'My soul magnifies the Lord, and my spirit rejoices in God my Savior, for he has looked on the humble estate of his servant. For behold, from now on all generations will call me blessed."

— Luke 1:46–48 (ESV)

EXPERIENCING THE STORY

Think about your relationship with God. Where is He asking you to surrender your plans to Him? What would it look like for you to embrace His plan for you?

Lesson 2

PURPOSE

Jesus was not just Mary's son,
He was something else. Something more.
— Jesus: His Life

They loved Him. She could see it in the eyes of the crowds as they hung on His every word. She could see it in the smiles of the sick He had miraculously healed. She could see it in the way His disciples followed Him. No, they didn't just love Him, they *worshiped* Him.

What she had known since before He was born and treasured in the silence of her own heart was now bursting into the world. Every mother thinks her child is special, but now she knew—her son was no ordinary man. He was the fulfillment of all her people's hopes and dreams. God's promises were brought to life in the form of her son, the boy she had watched grow from an infant in a manger to the man who stood before her.

Wherever He went, people followed. The blind saw; the lame were healed. To see God's promises fulfilled from so long ago was miraculous in and of itself, but to see them fulfilled in her own son ... What more could a mother desire? She had done what God asked her to do.

He was exactly who God promised He would be.

OPENING QUESTION

1. What's the best job or role you've ever had (paid or volunteer)? Why was it so fulfilling?

READING THE STORY

John 2:1–12 (NIV)

On the third day a wedding took place at Cana in Galilee. Jesus' mother was there, and Jesus and his disciples had also been invited to the wedding. When the wine was gone, Jesus' mother said to him, "They have no more wine." "Woman, why do you involve me?" Jesus replied. "My hour has not yet come." His mother said to the servants, "Do whatever he tells you." Nearby stood six stone water jars, the kind used by the Jews for ceremonial washing, each holding from twenty to thirty gallons. Jesus said to the servants, "Fill the jars with water"; so they filled them to the brim. Then he told them, "Now draw some out and take it to the master of the banquet." They did so, and the master of the banquet tasted the water that had been turned into wine. He did not realize where it had come from, though the servants who had drawn the water knew. Then he called the bridegroom aside and said, "Everyone brings out the choice wine first and then the cheaper wine after the guests have had too much to drink; but you have saved the best till now." What Jesus did here in Cana of Galilee was the first of the signs through which he revealed his glory; and his disciples believed in him. After this he went down to Capernaum with his mother and brothers and his disciples. There they stayed for a few days.

ENGAGING THE STORY

2. Why do you think Mary asked Jesus to help at the wedding? What do you think she expected to happen as a result of her request?

3. If you had been Mary, how might you have felt when Jesus called you "woman" (a respectful address, similar to "madam" or "ma'am") rather than mother?

4. What kind of relationship do you think Jesus had with His mother? How do you think He viewed Mary?

Jesus was changing, becoming stronger, bolder. News of her son would reach Mary. Strange stories that spoke of His powers increasing even further.
— Jesus: His Life

EXPLORING THE THEMES

Luke 2:48–52 (ESV)

And when his parents saw him, they were astonished. And his mother said to him, "Son, why have you treated us so? Behold, your father and I have been searching for you in great distress." And he said to them, "Why were you looking for me? Did you not know that I must be in my Father's house?" And they did not understand the saying that he spoke to them. And he went down with them and came to Nazareth and was submissive to them. And his mother treasured up all these things in her heart. And Jesus increased in wisdom and in stature and in favor with God and man.

John 19:26–27 (NIV)

When Jesus saw his mother there, and the disciple whom he loved standing nearby, he said to his mother, "Dear woman, here is your son," and to the disciple, "Here is your mother." From that time on, this disciple took her into his home.

Mary's son was the Messiah. Out of all the women in the world, God trusted her with His Son—trusted her to raise Him, to love Him, and to allow Him to be who God had called Him to be. Mary's mission, her calling, her purpose and destiny, was to raise and release Jesus. From the outside, it almost seemed mundane and insignificant. Her purpose was to be a mom. However, her faithfulness to the calling and purpose God gave her would have eternal impact.

It's easy for us to think our actions are insignificant. We're just a parent, we're just a man, just a woman, just a ______. Mary, however, reminds us that we aren't "just" anything. God has a plan and a purpose for each one of us!

5. Do you think only a few people have a purpose or a destiny, or that everyone has one? Why?

6. How do you think Mary felt about her calling as Jesus' mother when her son was mocked, attacked, and eventually crucified?

7. When have you seen something have a huge impact even though other people considered it insignificant? What happened?

Mary knew in this moment her mission was complete.
His purpose had only just begun.
— Jesus: His Life

EXPERIENCING THE STORY

What do you think God's purpose is for you in this season of your life? What has God asked you to do recently? How have you responded to His call?

Lesson 3
FAITH

Mary was proud that He saved people as He was destined to, but how would she explain that to His brothers and sisters?
— Jesus: His Life

The last time she held Him in her arms like this was that night in Bethlehem. He had looked so peaceful, even in the chaos of the stable. In spite of the blood and the wounds from the crown of thorns, He looked peaceful now as well. The long ordeal that had started in the early morning was finished.

The words she sang as a young girl echoed in her mind: "*All generations will call me blessed.*" Blessed? Far from it. No parent should have to hold their child's dead body. Had she failed? Should she have said something? Should she have warned Him as the opposition strengthened? He said He was the Messiah, and she had believed Him. But surely no true Messiah's life would end like this.

No. She knew what the angel had promised. "*He will reign over Israel forever.*" God had not failed. He kept His promises to Abraham, Isaac, and Jacob, and He would keep His promises to her. The sign they hung over Him said He was a king. He was.

The angel had promised His kingdom would have no end.

OPENING QUESTION

1. Think about a time when you were surprised by someone or something. What happened?

READING THE STORY

Luke 1:46–55 (NKJV)

And Mary said: "My soul magnifies the Lord,
And my spirit has rejoiced in God my Savior.
For He has regarded the lowly state of His maidservant;
For behold, henceforth all generations will call me blessed.
For He who is mighty has done great things for me,
And holy is His name.
And His mercy is on those who fear Him
From generation to generation.
He has shown strength with His arm;
He has scattered the proud in the imagination of their hearts.
He has put down the mighty from their thrones,
And exalted the lowly.
He has filled the hungry with good things,
And the rich He has sent away empty.
He has helped His servant Israel,
In remembrance of His mercy,
As He spoke to our fathers,
To Abraham and to his seed forever."

ENGAGING THE STORY

2. Mary sang this song when she first discovered she was pregnant with Jesus. How might her song have changed if she had known what would eventually happen to Jesus?

3. In her song, why do you think Mary refers to events that took place long before she was born? What impact do you think those events had on her relationship with God?

4. Why do you think Mary considered herself highly favored and blessed? If you had been in Mary's shoes, what words might you have used to describe yourself and your circumstances?

Mary knew Jesus from His first flutter of life.
She knows this is only the beginning.
— Jesus: His Life

EXPLORING THE THEMES

Mark 15:37–41 (NIV)

With a loud cry, Jesus breathed his last. The curtain of the temple was torn in two from top to bottom. And when the centurion, who stood there in front of Jesus, saw how he died, he said, "Surely this man was the Son of God!" Some women were watching from a distance. Among them were Mary Magdalene, Mary the mother of James the younger and of Joseph, and Salome. In Galilee these women had followed him and cared for his needs. Many other women who had come up with him to Jerusalem were also there.

Matthew 27:57–61 (NIV)

As evening approached, there came a rich man from Arimathea, named Joseph, who had himself become a disciple of Jesus. Going to Pilate, he asked for Jesus' body, and Pilate ordered that it be given to him. Joseph took the body, wrapped it in a clean linen cloth, and placed it in his own new tomb that he had cut out of the rock. He rolled a big stone in front of the entrance to the tomb and went away. Mary Magdalene and the other Mary were sitting there opposite the tomb.

As she cradled her son's body in her arms, Mary must have thought back to the promise the angel had given her before Jesus was born. Her son was going to rescue His people from their sins. From where Mary sat, it must have looked like God had failed to keep His promise.

Yet, God didn't fail. Three days later God proved that Jesus was exactly who He said He was—the Messiah, the promised king who would rescue humanity from the power of sin, death, and evil. As God had done so many other times in Mary's life, He kept His promise. Just like Mary, we can be confident that God will keep His promises to us. That's the essence of faith—a confidence that God will keep His promises.

5. Describe a time in your life when someone kept a promise you thought was impossible for them to keep. How did that affect your relationship with the person?

6. How do you respond to God when it seems like He hasn't kept a promise to you? How does this affect your view of God and your relationship with Him?

7. Why do you think God allows us to experience times where it seems like He has forgotten His promises to us?

Mary will wait, endure, and pray. She is His mother, and when the time comes, she'll be there.

—Jesus: His Life

EXPERIENCING THE STORY

Reflect on your life story to now. When has God kept His promises to you? When has it seemed like God has forgotten His promises to you? How would a firm confidence in God (and His promises) change your relationship with Him?

EPISODE 4

CAIAPHAS

Lesson 1: Power

Lesson 2: Anger

Lesson 3: Choice

Lesson 1
POWER

Could Caiaphas have acted differently from the start? Probably. Did he underestimate Jesus? Certainly.

— Jesus: His Life

Caiaphas was starting to grow concerned. This Jesus was becoming a problem. There were always deranged men who wandered the deserts claiming they had a message from God. So long as they stayed in the deserts, they weren't a problem.

Jesus refused to stay in the desert. He and His band of followers had come to the populated areas, disrupting events at the Temple, making outrageous claims—all actions that would bring the attention of Rome. Roman attention was something Caiaphas would do anything to avoid, as Roman attention usually resulted in blood at best, and burned cities and mass crucifixions at worst.

This Jesus had no idea what kind of effort Caiaphas exerted to maintain the small sliver of independence Israel enjoyed; His actions threatened to disrupt the balance of power Caiaphas had so carefully constructed. While Jesus was healing beggars in the streets, Caiaphas was protecting his people. So long as Jesus didn't create too much of a commotion, Caiaphas would allow Him to continue.

But he would not let Jesus destroy everything he had worked so hard to create.

OPENING QUESTION

1. Who is the most influential person you've ever met? How did you meet them?

READING THE STORY

John 9:13–17 (ESV)

They brought to the Pharisees the man who had formerly been blind. Now it was a Sabbath day when Jesus made the mud and opened his eyes. So the Pharisees again asked him how he had received his sight. And he said to them, "He put mud on my eyes, and I washed, and I see." Some of the Pharisees said, "This man is not from God, for he does not keep the Sabbath." But others said, "How can a man who is a sinner do such signs?" And there was a division among them. So they said again to the blind man, "What do you say about him, since he has opened your eyes?" He said, "He is a prophet."

ENGAGING THE STORY

2. If you saw a man who was blind from birth but who had been miraculously healed, how would you respond? What would you think about the person who healed the blind man?

3. Why do you think the Pharisees felt threatened by Jesus' healing of the blind man?

4. Why do you think the Pharisees did not acknowledge that Jesus was from God?

Caiaphas was in charge of keeping the peace and stability in Judea. No one will be able to say Caiaphas did nothing.

—Jesus: His Life

EXPLORING THE THEMES

Matthew 23:1–7 (ESV)

Then Jesus said to the crowds and to his disciples, "The scribes and the Pharisees sit on Moses' seat, so do and observe whatever they tell you, but not the works they do. For they preach, but do not practice. They tie up heavy burdens, hard to bear, and lay them on people›s shoulders, but they themselves are not willing to move them with their finger. They do all their deeds to be seen by others. For they make their phylacteries broad and their fringes long, and they love the place of honor at feasts and the best seats in the synagogues and greetings in the market-places and being called rabbi by others."

Jesus threatened the power of the priests and Pharisees. He announced a new way of relating to God. The Pharisees and priests also had the difficult job of protecting the Temple and maintaining the delicate peace between disparate groups and factions in Jerusalem. Through His teaching and His actions, Jesus upended the system they thought was important and replaced it with something different—a kingdom centered on Him.

Jesus continues that same work today. He challenges the things we think are important—power, position, prestige, and possessions—and replaces them with His eternal kingdom.

For now things are peaceful.
But Caiaphas knew just how quickly that can change.
— Jesus: His Life

5. Why do you think the Pharisees' actions were so frustrating to Jesus?

6. Why did the Pharisees think they were powerful? Why do you think many people believe they're powerful today?

7. How was Jesus' power different from that of the Pharisees? How did Jesus demonstrate His power? How does Jesus demonstrate His power today?

EXPERIENCING THE STORY

Think about your life. What "power" (position, prestige, possessions, etc.) do you value? Where does your faith and your relationship with Jesus rank among your priorities? What difference could it make for you to embrace Jesus' power rather than any other power you value? What would it take for you to do this?

Lesson 2

ANGER

Jesus grew bolder. He kept coming to the city,
and He had a reputation as a healer.
— Jesus: His Life

Jesus had gone too far! The incident with Lazarus had crossed a line. Healings and other miracles happened all the time, but this—this was a *threat*. News would spread, people would talk, and Jesus and His followers would only grow bolder, which would attract Roman attention. Caiaphas couldn't allow that.

Who did Jesus think He was anyway? He had no education and no rabbinical training; He was a carpenter! It burned Caiaphas to see the people hanging on to everything He said. Jesus knew nothing about Caiaphas' efforts to stay in Rome's good graces and to protect the nation of Israel.

If Jesus' popularity continued to rise, if His followers grew more bold in publicly claiming He was the Messiah, Rome would respond with violence against Jerusalem. Caiaphas had been patient and had tolerated Jesus' disruptions and accusations, but no more.

Jesus had to be stopped.

OPENING QUESTION

1. What's the most outrageous story a friend has ever told you? How did you react to the story?

READING THE STORY

John 11:43–53 (NIV)

When he had said this, Jesus called in a loud voice, "Lazarus, come out!" The dead man came out, his hands and feet wrapped with strips of linen, and a cloth around his face. Jesus said to them, "Take off the grave clothes and let him go." Many of the Jews therefore, who had come with Mary and had seen what he did, believed in him, but some of them went to the Pharisees and told them what Jesus had done. So the chief priests and the Pharisees gathered the council and said, "What are we to do? For this man performs many signs. If we let him go on like this, everyone will believe in him, and the Romans will come and take away both our place and our nation." But one of them, Caiaphas, who was high priest that year, said to them, "You know nothing at all. Nor do you understand that it is better for you that one man should die for the people, not that the whole nation should perish." He did not say this of his own accord, but being high priest that year he prophesied that Jesus would die for the nation, and not for the nation only, but also to gather into one the children of God who are scattered abroad. So from that day on they made plans to put him to death.

ENGAGING THE STORY

2. Jesus had done other miraculous things before. Why do you think raising Lazarus from the dead made Caiaphas and the other priests so upset?

3. Why do you think Caiaphas and the other priests might have had a hard time believing Jesus actually raised Lazarus from the dead?

4. Why did Caiaphas want Jesus dead? What do you think Caiaphas hoped Jesus' death would accomplish for him? For Israel?

If so many could be taken in by His tricks,
Caiaphas couldn't ignore Him.
— Jesus: His Life

EXPLORING THE THEMES

Mark 11:15–18 (NIV)

On reaching Jerusalem, Jesus entered the temple courts and began driving out those who were buying and selling there. He overturned the tables of the money changers and the benches of those selling doves, and would not allow anyone to carry merchandise through the temple courts. And as he taught them, he said, "Is it not written: 'My house will be called a house of prayer for all nations'? But you have made it 'a den of robbers.'" The chief priests and the teachers of the law heard this and began looking for a way to kill him, for they feared him, because the whole crowd was amazed at his teaching.

Matthew 21:45–46 (NIV)

When the chief priests and the Pharisees heard Jesus' parables, they knew he was talking about them. They looked for a way to arrest him, but they were afraid of the crowd because the people held that he was a prophet.

When He raised Lazarus from the dead, it was as if Jesus signed His own death warrant. He had done something the priests couldn't ignore; they *had* to respond to this incident. Every action, every story, and every miracle Jesus performed increased their anger. Jesus was a threat to the nation, yes, but He was a threat to them as well.

Jesus is the only Way anyone can get to God. Only He can rescue us from the brokenness of the world around us. Meaning is found in serving, rather than being served. Only those who lose their lives will experience real life. These claims threaten us personally. If they are true, it means we must live, think, and act differently.

5. What did Jesus do and say that made the priests and Pharisees so angry?

6. What are some of the ways you've seen people respond to the hard, provocative claims and statements Jesus makes?

7. Why do you think people can become angry when they hear Jesus' teachings?

"When the chief priests and the Pharisees heard Jesus' parables, they knew he was talking about them."
— Matthew 21:45 (NIV)

EXPERIENCING THE STORY

Which of Jesus' teachings do you find difficult or challenging? Why do they challenge you? Related to those teachings, how do you try to maintain what you want rather than following what Jesus has said? What would it look like for you to embrace Jesus' teachings rather than trying to do away with them?

Lesson 3
CHOICE

To Caiaphas, Jesus was just a man—flesh and blood—
and Caiaphas would not be afraid of him.
— Jesus: His Life

Caiaphas finally stood face-to-face with the man who had caused him so many problems. Jesus stood in the middle of the room as the council prepared to decide His fate. Not that there was any doubt about the outcome of the trial. Caiaphas and the other leaders knew what had to happen. They had already made their decision.

Would some condemn Caiaphas for his actions? Yes, of course. But they didn't see what he saw. If Jesus were allowed to continue preaching and teaching there would be swift and inevitable judgment from Rome. The life of one man was a small price to pay for peace. Jesus and His followers claimed He was the long-awaited Messiah—that He was the king promised by the prophets long ago. But this carpenter was not, and could not be, the Messiah!

He would show everyone who this Jesus really was.

OPENING QUESTION

1. What is the most difficult choice you've had to make in the last month? How did you decide what to do?

READING THE STORY

Matthew 26:59–66 (NIV)

The chief priests and the whole Sanhedrin were looking for false evidence against Jesus so that they could put him to death. But they did not find any, though many false witnesses came forward. Finally two came forward and declared, "This fellow said, 'I am able to destroy the temple of God and rebuild it in three days.'" Then the high priest stood up and said to Jesus, "Are you not going to answer? What is this testimony that these men are bringing against you?" But Jesus remained silent. The high priest said to him, "I charge you under oath by the living God: Tell us if you are the Messiah, the Son of God." "You have said so," Jesus replied. "But I say to all of you: From now on you will see the Son of Man sitting at the right hand of the Mighty One and coming on the clouds of heaven." Then the high priest tore his clothes and said, "He has spoken blasphemy! Why do we need any more witnesses? Look, now you have heard the blasphemy. What do you think?" "He is worthy of death," they answered.

ENGAGING THE STORY

2. Why do you think Caiaphas and the Sanhedrin chose to accuse Jesus of blasphemy?

3. If Caiaphas and the other Jewish leaders had already decided Jesus must die, why do you think they decided to put Jesus on trial?

4. What could Jesus have said or done that might have changed Caiaphas' plans?

Caiaphas knew He was dangerous.

—Jesus: His Life

EXPLORING THE THEMES

Luke 22:66–68 (NIV)

At daybreak the council of the elders of the people, both the chief priests and the teachers of the law, met together, and Jesus was led before them. "If you are the Messiah," they said, "tell us." Jesus answered, "If I tell you, you will not believe me, and if I asked you, you would not answer."

Luke 23:1–2 (NIV)

Then the whole assembly rose and led him off to Pilate. And they began to accuse him, saying, "We have found this man subverting our nation. He opposes payment of taxes to Caesar and claims to be Messiah, a king."

Caiaphas and the Sanhedrin had made up their minds. They decided Jesus was a heretic and a threat. He had to be stopped. Jesus had made His choices—to raise Lazarus, to disrupt the Temple, to refuse to walk away—and Caiaphas had made his choice. It would not end well for Jesus. There was no going back.

To Caiaphas,
Jesus must be stopped. No matter what.
— Jesus: His Life

5. Why do you think the members of the council chose to take Jesus to Pilate?

6. What do you think Jesus knew about the members of the council when He refused to answer (or to clearly answer) their questions?

7. Why do you think the Jewish religious leaders chose to reject Jesus as their King? Why do you think some people choose to reject Jesus today?

EXPERIENCING THE STORY

What choices is God asking you to make right now? What options do you have? How might it affect your life if you chose to do what God asks? What about if you chose not to do what God says?

EPISODE 5

JUDAS ISCARIOT

Lesson 1: Rejection

Lesson 2: Betrayal

Lesson 3: Regret

Lesson 1
REJECTION

Judas didn't fit in with the rest of the disciples.
He felt invisible to them.
— Jesus: His Life

Judas. Even today, two thousand years later, his name is synonymous with betrayal. In art, literature, and poetry, Judas is portrayed as the ultimate villain—the man who handed the Son of God over to be tortured and crucified.

Even so, Judas' motives for betraying Jesus are quite a mystery. The questions that surround Jesus' betrayal aren't related to "who?" but instead are all about "why?"

Why would Judas, who had given up three years of his life to follow Jesus, betray Him? What could possibly motivate Judas to such treachery against the man he loved and loyally followed? Why would he choose to reject the man who had impacted his life and given him a new purpose and calling? How could Judas possibly turn on Jesus and repay His kindness and friendship with betrayal?

We may never know for sure, but as we take a detailed look at Judas, we see more than a cartoon villain. We see an outsider, a loner, the only disciple who was from southern Israel. While Judas' choice to betray Jesus was evil, he must have somehow rationalized his actions. Is it possible that Judas' misguided feelings of rejection affected not only his relationships but also his decisions?

OPENING QUESTION

1. Have you ever played a game where you picked teams beforehand? How did that process make you feel (or how do you think it would make you feel)?

READING THE STORY

John 12:1–8 (NKJV)

Then, six days before the Passover, Jesus came to Bethany, where Lazarus was who had been dead, whom He had raised from the dead. There they made Him a supper; and Martha served, but Lazarus was one of those who sat at the table with Him. Then Mary took a pound of very costly oil of spikenard, anointed the feet of Jesus, and wiped His feet with her hair. And the house was filled with the fragrance of the oil.

But one of His disciples, Judas Iscariot, Simon's son, who would betray Him, said, "Why was this fragrant oil not sold for three hundred denarii and given to the poor?" This he said, not that he cared for the poor, but because he was a thief, and had the money box; and he used to take what was put in it.

But Jesus said, "Let her alone; she has kept this for the day of My burial. For the poor you have with you always, but Me you do not have always."

ENGAGING THE STORY

2. Do you think Judas was an outsider compared to the rest of the disciples? Why or why not?

3. Why do you think Jesus corrected Judas as He did in the passage above? If you had been in Judas' shoes, how would Jesus' correction have made you feel? Why would you feel that way?

4. Judas perceived that Jesus and the other disciples had rejected him. How do you think this influenced his relationships with them?

"If your brother or sister sins, go and point out their fault,
just between the two of you.
If they listen to you, you have won them over."
— Matthew 18:15 (NIV)

EXPLORING THE THEMES

Matthew 10:1–4 (ESV)

And he called to him his twelve disciples and gave them authority over unclean spirits, to cast them out, and to heal every disease and every affliction. The names of the twelve apostles are these: first, Simon, who is called Peter, and Andrew his brother; James the son of Zebedee, and John his brother; Philip and Bartholomew; Thomas and Matthew the tax collector; James the son of Alphaeus, and Thaddaeus; Simon the Zealot, and Judas Iscariot, who betrayed him.

John 6:66–71 (ESV)

After this many of his disciples turned back and no longer walked with him. So Jesus said to the twelve, "Do you want to go away as well?" Simon Peter answered him, "Lord, to whom shall we go? You have the words of eternal life, and we have believed, and have come to know, that you are the Holy One of God." Jesus answered them, "Did I not choose you, the twelve? And yet one of you is a devil." He spoke of Judas the son of Simon Iscariot, for he, one of the twelve, was going to betray him.

We've all had moments where we felt like outsiders—like we didn't belong or couldn't really connect with anyone. In Judas' mind, that perceived rejection might have justified his betrayal of Jesus. When we feel rejected by someone or by a group, we can start to view everything others do through the lens of our feelings. Thus we use our hurt and pain to justify attitudes and actions that we would otherwise never embrace.

When someone hurts us, we might feel like we want to hurt other people. We might want others to feel the pain we feel, especially if they caused our hurt. Other times we bury our pain and let it fester. The good news is, Jesus gives us a better way to resolve feelings of pain and rejection! Rather than lashing out or bottling up our feelings, Jesus gives us the tools to reconcile with people and forgive them. Forgiveness, somehow, has the ability to heal us.

5. When a person is rejected by a person or a group, what feelings do you think they experience?

6. Which is your go-to response when you get hurt by someone—lashing out or bottling up? How does that influence how you interact with the one(s) who hurt you?

7. How do you think the story might have been different if Judas hadn't let his feelings of rejection control him?

Peter's blind faith filled Judas' heart with envy.
It was all so easy for Peter.
— Jesus: His Life

EXPERIENCING THE STORY

Think about your relationships. Is there anyone who has rejected or hurt you? Do you have feelings you've bottled up or used as an excuse to lash out? Take some time to pray about them and ask God to help you share those feelings in a way that leads to reconciliation, rather than rejection.

Lesson 2
BETRAYAL

If Jesus knew what Judas was about to do,
why didn't Jesus stop him?
— Jesus: His Life

On the night before Jesus' crucifixion, He celebrated the Passover meal with His disciples. During the meal, Jesus washed the disciples' feet, giving them an example of sacrificial love. As the group ate and drank, the joy of Passover diminished as Jesus began to talk about His upcoming death. The mood in the room shifted from levity to somber confusion.

To make matters worse, halfway through the meal, Jesus announced that one of the disciples in the room would betray Him. One of the men who had spent the last three years walking with Him, serving with Him, and learning from Him would turn on Him and bring about His death.

The disciples must have first been horrified and then suspicious! How could one of them do such a thing? And if so, who was it? Surely Jesus must be joking or speaking in riddles like He did so many other times. Imagine their dismay when they found out it was Judas. His betrayal had such tragic consequences. And now that Jesus was dead, they were afraid and hiding. They may have looked around the room at the other disciples and wondered to themselves, "Who else will betray us?"

OPENING QUESTION

1. Why is betrayal such a painful experience?

READING THE STORY

John 13:21–30 (ESV)

After saying these things, Jesus was troubled in his spirit, and testified, "Truly, truly, I say to you, one of you will betray me." The disciples looked at one another, uncertain of whom he spoke. One of his disciples, whom Jesus loved, was reclining at table at Jesus' side, so Simon Peter motioned to him to ask Jesus of whom he was speaking. So that disciple, leaning back against Jesus, said to him, "Lord, who is it?" Jesus answered, "It is he to whom I will give this morsel of bread when I have dipped it." So when he had dipped the morsel, he gave it to Judas, the son of Simon Iscariot. Then after he had taken the morsel, Satan entered into him. Jesus said to him, "What you are going to do, do quickly." Now no one at the table knew why he said this to him. Some thought that, because Judas had the moneybag, Jesus was telling him, "Buy what we need for the feast," or that he should give something to the poor. So, after receiving the morsel of bread, he immediately went out. And it was night.

ENGAGING THE STORY

2. Even though Jesus knew Judas would betray Him, Jesus still trusted Judas and had a relationship with him. If you had been in Jesus' shoes, how would you have interacted with Judas?

3. If you had been one of the disciples, how would Jesus' announcement (that someone in the room would betray Him) make you feel? What might you have thought when Judas left the room?

4. Do you think the other disciples expected Judas to betray Jesus? Why or why not? How do you think they felt after they realized what Judas had done?

"During supper, when the devil had already put it into the heart of Judas Iscariot, Simon's son, to betray him . . ."
— John 13:2 (ESV)

EXPLORING THE THEMES

John 13:1–5 (ESV)

Now before the Feast of the Passover, when Jesus knew that his hour had come to depart out of this world to the Father, having loved his own who were in the world, he loved them to the end. During supper, when the devil had already put it into the heart of Judas Iscariot, Simon's son, to betray him, Jesus, knowing that the Father had given all things into his hands, and that he had come from God and was going back to God, rose from supper. He laid aside his outer garments, and taking a towel, tied it around his waist. Then he poured water into a basin and began to wash the disciples' feet and to wipe them with the towel that was wrapped around him.

Mark 14:17–21 (NIV)

When evening came, Jesus arrived with the Twelve. While they were reclining at the table eating, he said, "Truly I tell you, one of you will betray me—one who is eating with me." They were saddened, and one by one they said to him, "Surely you don't mean me?" "It is one of the Twelve," he replied, "one who dips bread into the bowl with me. The Son of Man will go just as it is written about him. But woe to that man who betrays the Son of Man! It would be better for him if he had not been born."

When the other disciples realized what Judas had done, they may have thought of the other disciples and wondered, "Who else can I *not* trust?" That's why betrayal is so painful. It doesn't just damage our relationship with the person who betrayed us, it also plants the seeds of doubt in every other relationship we have. We start to wonder, "Can I really trust this person?" "Will they hurt me like other people have?"

The good news is that even though people may hurt us and make it hard for us to trust, as believers, we serve a God who will never let us down! Jesus was rejected, betrayed, and killed. He knows the pain we feel when we are treated that way too. But we also have hope that God doesn't abandon us. Rather He comes to rescue us.

5. How do you think you would feel if you were betrayed by someone close to you?

6. What impact do you think betrayal has on a relationship between two people? How do you think that betrayal impacts their other relationships?

7. Why do you think Jesus was able to wash Judas' feet, even though He knew what Judas was about to do?

EXPERIENCING THE STORY

Think about your story. When have you been hurt or betrayed by people you love? How has that affected your ability to trust other people? If God suddenly healed those wounds and restored your trust, how would your relationships be different?

Lesson 3
REGRET

Judas realized he had played right into their hands. This would be his legacy; he was the man who handed Jesus to His executioners.

— Jesus: His Life

With a simple kiss, Judas handed Jesus over to the men who would eventually have Jesus killed. Judas had made his decision, played his part in the High Priest's plan, and received his reward. Even so, he was shaken by the events that unfolded after his betrayal. Jesus was put on trial, but the guilty verdict had been determined before the trial even started. As Jesus was led away to the place of His execution, Judas realized he had made a mistake.

Judas had a sickening realization—he had betrayed an innocent man. Jesus would soon be crucified as a direct result of Judas' actions. There was nothing Judas could do to reverse the events he had set in motion. Jesus' execution couldn't be stopped.

Judas tried to ease his guilt by returning the money the High Priest had paid him, but it didn't help. For the rest of history, his name would be synonymous with betrayal. He would be remembered as the man who betrayed Jesus. There was no going back, no changing what had been done.

OPENING QUESTION

1. Have you ever made a decision you later regretted? What happened?

READING THE STORY

Mark 14:43–50 (NKJV)

And immediately, while He was still speaking, Judas, one of the twelve, with a great multitude with swords and clubs, came from the chief priests and the scribes and the elders. Now His betrayer had given them a signal, saying, "Whomever I kiss, He is the One; seize Him and lead Him away safely." As soon as he had come, immediately he went up to Him and said to Him, "Rabbi, Rabbi!" and kissed Him. Then they laid their hands on Him and took Him. And one of those who stood by drew his sword and struck the servant of the high priest, and cut off his ear. Then Jesus answered and said to them, "Have you come out, as against a robber, with swords and clubs to take Me? I was daily with you in the temple teaching, and you did not seize Me. But the Scriptures must be fulfilled." Then they all forsook Him and fled.

ENGAGING THE STORY

2. How do you think Judas felt when He saw Jesus arrested? How do you think he felt after Jesus was taken away?

3. Judas seemed confident in his decision to betray Jesus until He was sentenced to death. What do you think made Judas re-evaluate his actions?

4. Do you think Judas was genuinely repentant for betraying Jesus? Why or why not?

"And immediately, while He was still speaking, Judas, one of the twelve, with a great multitude with swords and clubs, came from the chief priests and the scribes and the elders."

— Mark 14:43 (NKJV)

EXPLORING THE THEMES

Luke 22:47–48 (NIV)

While he was still speaking a crowd came up, and the man who was called Judas, one of the Twelve, was leading them. He approached Jesus to kiss him, but Jesus asked him, "Judas, are you betraying the Son of Man with a kiss?"

Matthew 27:3–5 (NIV)

When Judas, who had betrayed him, saw that Jesus was condemned, he was seized with remorse and returned the thirty pieces of silver to the chief priests and the elders. "I have sinned," he said, "for I have betrayed innocent blood." "What is that to us?" they replied. "That's your responsibility." So Judas threw the money into the temple and left. Then he went away and hanged himself.

When Judas recognized what he had done—that he had handed Jesus over to His executioners—he was overwhelmed with remorse and regret. He tried to fix what he had done by returning the money the High Priest paid him to betray Jesus, but that didn't make the feelings of anguish and failure go away. In Judas' mind, the only option was to kill himself.

We all have regrets. There are decisions we wish we had made differently and words we wish we could take back. When we think about all the mistakes we've made and regrets we have, it can leave us feeling overwhelmed. We may feel like we're terrible people—beyond any hope of redemption. The good news of Jesus, however, is that none of us are too far gone; there's no sin or mistake Jesus can't forgive!

5. What are some of the most common regrets people have in their lives? How do you think most people handle their regrets?

6. Do you think there is a decision or mistake God can't or won't forgive? Why or why not?

7. How could Judas have handled his regret differently?

Judas wished he could go back to those precious months when he first knew Jesus.
— Jesus: His Life

EXPERIENCING THE STORY

Think about your life. What regrets do you have? If you could go back and do things differently in your career, relationships, finances, or other areas, what would you change? What can you do now to make things different or better?

EPISODE 6

PILATE

Lesson 1: Truth

Lesson 2: Responsibility

Lesson 3: Control

Lesson 1
TRUTH

What accusations do you bring against this man?
— Jesus: His Life

Pilate wanted to be anywhere other than Jerusalem. Jerusalem was an insignificant town on the fringes of the empire, far removed from the glory and power of Rome. Worse, he saw the inhabitants of Jerusalem as strange people with strange customs—and they stubbornly held to those customs, no matter what kind of trouble it caused. In Pilate's mind, his job was simple: keep the peace and do it well enough to earn a promotion that would take him elsewhere.

That was easier said than done. Passover always seemed to increase the tension in Jerusalem. Rebels always popped up and made their move as thousands streamed into the city to make sacrifices.

This year was no different. It was only early morning, but the priests had already hauled another revolutionary with dreams of overthrowing Rome in front of him. Normally it would be a quick decision—another example of why threatening Rome was a recipe for a painful death—but this one was . . . different. No threats, no resistance. This wasn't a normal trial. There was much more at stake, more behind the priest's claim that this man had tried to overthrow Caesar.

Who was this Jesus?

OPENING QUESTION

1. Who was Jesus to those around Him? Who is Jesus to you?

READING THE STORY

John 18:33–37 (NKJV)

Then Pilate entered the Praetorium again, called Jesus, and said to Him, "Are You the King of the Jews?" Jesus answered him, "Are you speaking for yourself about this, or did others tell you this concerning Me?" Pilate answered, "Am I a Jew? Your own nation and the chief priests have delivered You to me. What have You done?" Jesus answered, "My kingdom is not of this world. If My kingdom were of this world, My servants would fight, so that I should not be delivered to the Jews; but now My kingdom is not from here." Pilate therefore said to Him, "Are You a king then?" Jesus answered, "You say rightly that I am a king. For this cause I was born, and for this cause I have come into the world, that I should bear witness to the truth. Everyone who is of the truth hears My voice."

ENGAGING THE STORY

2. Why do you think Pilate was so confused by Jesus' answers to his questions?

3. If you had been Pilate, what might you have thought when Jesus told you He was a king?

4. The chief priests didn't like the sign Pilate later placed above Jesus on the cross, which indicated Jesus was the King of the Jews (John 19:21). Why do you think their responses regarding Jesus' kingship were so different?

Is this Jesus really the danger they say He is?

—Jesus: His Life

EXPLORING THE THEMES

Luke 23:1–2 (NKJV)

Then the whole multitude of them arose and led Him to Pilate. And they began to accuse Him, saying, "We found this fellow perverting the nation, and forbidding to pay taxes to Caesar, saying that He Himself is Christ, a King."

John 18:38 (NKJV)

Pilate said to Him, "What is truth?" And when he had said this, he went out again to the Jews, and said to them, "I find no fault in Him at all."

Jesus' life hung on a single question: whose view of Him was true? Was the priests' claim that He was a rebel bent on overthrowing Rome true, or was Jesus something—someone—different? Was He just an unusual holy man? Who was Jesus?

Pilate had to answer that question, and so do we. Whose view of Jesus is true? Is Jesus just a good person who was killed by people who didn't understand Him, or is He something more? Our answer to this question will determine so much about our lives and our eternities.

"Then Pilate entered the Praetorium again, called Jesus, and said to Him, "Are You the King of the Jews?"

— John 18:33 (NKJV)

5. What are your thoughts when you hear the word "truth"? Why do you think that way?

6. Why do you think Pilate asked Jesus, "What is truth?" How would you answer his question?

7. Pilate and the priests responded differently to Jesus' claim to be a king. What are some ways people respond to Jesus today?

EXPERIENCING THE STORY

If someone were to ask you the question "Who is Jesus?" what would you say? How does your life support your answer?

Lesson 2
RESPONSIBILITY

There was enough scandal attached to Pilate's name.
He wanted no part of this.
— Jesus: His Life

Things were not going as planned. What should have been a quick and simple decision to execute an annoying rabble-rouser had spiraled out of control. Who was this Jesus? The priests were insistent that He was a traitor, a threat to Rome, a revolutionary who must be stopped at all costs. There must have been something else Caiaphas and the other priests were plotting.

Pilate was just as strategic and political as Caiaphas. Pilate knew Jesus had amassed quite the following. Just a few days earlier the entire city had given Jesus a hero's welcome as He entered Jerusalem. Who knew what His followers would do if Jesus was hanged on a cross outside the city gate? A riot followed by a rebellion and a massacre was not how Pilate would gain the Emperor's favor. He suspected the chief priests were trying to make him do their dirty work. Was that what the priests had in mind? Was this a move to push Pilate out of Jerusalem?

What Pilate really needed was a way to solve this Jesus problem without getting personally involved. Who could he make responsible for dealing with this supposed king?

OPENING QUESTION

1. Do you consider yourself to be a decisive person or indecisive person? How easy is it for you to make decisions?

READING THE STORY

Luke 23:6–12 (ESV)

When Pilate heard this, he asked whether the man was a Galilean. And when he learned that he belonged to Herod's jurisdiction, he sent him over to Herod, who was himself in Jerusalem at that time. When Herod saw Jesus, he was very glad, for he had long desired to see him, because he had heard about him, and he was hoping to see some sign done by him. So he questioned him at some length, but he made no answer. The chief priests and the scribes stood by, vehemently accusing him. And Herod with his soldiers treated him with contempt and mocked him. Then, arraying him in splendid clothing, he sent him back to Pilate. And Herod and Pilate became friends with each other that very day, for before this they had been at enmity with each other.

Pilate would use their own customs to settle their dispute.

— Jesus: His Life

ENGAGING THE STORY

2. Why do you think Pilate sent Jesus to Herod? Why do you think Pilate was unwilling to make a decision about Jesus by himself?

3. Why you think Herod's attitude about Jesus quickly changed from anticipation to disrespect?

4. What evidence is there that Pilate and Herod were indecisive and weak leaders?

EXPLORING THE THEMES

Luke 23:13–23 (ESV)

Then Pilate, when he had called together the chief priests, the rulers, and the people, said to them, "You have brought this Man to me, as one who misleads the people. And indeed, having examined Him in your presence, I have found no fault in this Man concerning those things of which you accuse Him; no, neither did Herod, for I sent you back to him; and indeed nothing deserving of death has been done by Him. I will therefore chastise Him and release Him" (for it was necessary for him to release one to them at the feast). And they all cried out at once, saying, "Away with this Man, and release to us Barabbas"—who had been thrown into prison for a certain rebellion made in the city, and for murder. Pilate, therefore, wishing to release Jesus, again called out to them. But they shouted, saying, "Crucify Him, crucify Him!" Then he said to them the third time, "Why, what evil has He done? I have found no reason for death in Him. I will therefore chastise Him and let Him go." But they were insistent, demanding with loud voices that He be crucified. And the voices of these men and of the chief priests prevailed.

Matthew 27:24–26 (ESV)

So when Pilate saw that he was gaining nothing, but rather that a riot was beginning, he took water and washed his hands before the crowd, saying, "I am innocent of this man's blood; see to it yourselves." And all the people answered, "His blood be on us and on our children!" Then he released for them Barabbas, and having scourged Jesus, delivered him to be crucified.

Jesus had confronted the leaders and rulers of Jerusalem and accused them of wrongdoing. A challenge like that couldn't be ignored, but no one wanted to take responsibility for it. The priests, Pilate, and Herod all viewed Jesus as a problem someone else needed to solve, even though they saw Him as a threat to their positions, power, and influence. Jesus had to be dealt with, but no one wanted to be the one who made the final decision.

At some point, all of us will experience a moment like this—a moment when Jesus confronts us, challenges our thinking and actions, and threatens the way we view the world, ourselves, and God. Our temptation in those times is to let someone else deal with Jesus and insist that we aren't responsible; He is someone else's problem.

5. Why do you think Pilate and Herod both refused to make a decision about Jesus? How do you think this impacted their relationship with the priests? How do you think it impacted their relationship with God?

6. Why would the priests and Pilate have considered Jesus a threat? Would Jesus be perceived as a threat today?

7. What does it mean for someone to take responsibility for their relationship with Jesus? What does this involve?

They wanted Pilate to do their dirty work.

—Jesus: His Life

EXPERIENCING THE STORY

How is Jesus challenging the way you think, act, or feel? How might responding to His challenge take your relationship with Him to a new level? How can you take more responsibility for your relationship with God?

Lesson 3
CONTROL

What was another dead man to Pilate? Golgotha was soaked in the blood of countless men who no one remembered.

— Jesus: His Life

This had gone too far. Herod had refused to handle Jesus, so it fell to Pilate to clean up the mess before things really got out of hand. Fine. He had been a soldier, so it didn't bother him to kill. Jesus would become just another one of the countless rebels and zealots who had crossed Rome and paid the price.

Yes, Caiaphas and his ilk wanted Jesus dead for their own reasons, but they didn't have the power to do it. Rome was the ultimate power in the world, and Jesus would serve as another bloody example to drive home that point to everyone in Jerusalem. This was no longer about whatever squabbles Jesus had instigated; it was now about demonstrating Rome's power and control.

Jesus, Caiaphas, and Herod were all under Caesar's control. The only power they had was that which Rome had given them, and Pilate distributed that power. They said Jesus was a king, but there was only one king.

Pilate would show them who was really in charge.

OPENING QUESTION

1. In your opinion, who is the most powerful person, or what is the most powerful group, in the world? Why do you think this?

READING THE STORY

John 19:5–12 (NIV)

When Jesus came out wearing the crown of thorns and the purple robe, Pilate said to them, "Here is the man!" As soon as the chief priests and their officials saw him, they shouted, "Crucify! Crucify!" But Pilate answered, "You take him and crucify him. As for me, I find no basis for a charge against him." The Jewish leaders insisted, "We have a law, and according to that law he must die, because he claimed to be the Son of God." Therefore, when Pilate heard that saying, he was the more afraid, and went again into the Praetorium, and said to Jesus, "Where are You from?" But Jesus gave him no answer. Then Pilate said to Him, "Are You not speaking to me? Do You not know that I have power to crucify You, and power to release You?" Jesus answered, "You could have no power at all against Me unless it had been given you from above. Therefore the one who delivered Me to you has the greater sin." From then on Pilate sought to release Him, but the Jews cried out, saying, "If you let this Man go, you are not Caesar's friend. Whoever makes himself a king speaks against Caesar."

ENGAGING THE STORY

2. If you had been Pilate, how would you have responded when Jesus insisted you had no power except what had been given you from above? Why would you respond that way?

3. Why do you think Pilate agreed to crucify Jesus even though he wanted to release Jesus?

4. Why do you think Pilate was afraid when he heard Jesus claimed to be the Son of God? If this were true, what would it indicate about who was really in control of the situation?

Rome wouldn't waste a second thought on Jesus,
so why should Pilate?
— Jesus: His Life

EXPLORING THE THEMES

John 19:17–22 (NKJV)

And He, bearing His cross, went out to a place called the Place of a Skull, which is called in Hebrew, Golgotha, where they crucified Him, and two others with Him, one on either side, and Jesus in the center. Now Pilate wrote a title and put it on the cross. And the writing was: JESUS OF NAZARETH, THE KING OF THE JEWS. Then many of the Jews read this title, for the place where Jesus was crucified was near the city; and it was written in Hebrew, Greek, and Latin. Therefore the chief priests of the Jews said to Pilate, "Do not write, 'The King of the Jews,' but, 'He said, "I am the King of the Jews." ' " Pilate answered, "What I have written, I have written."

Colossians 2:13–15 (NKJV)

And you, being dead in your trespasses and the uncircumcision of your flesh, He has made alive together with Him, having forgiven you all trespasses, having wiped out the handwriting of requirements that was against us, which was contrary to us. And He has taken it out of the way, having nailed it to the cross. Having disarmed principalities and powers, He made a public spectacle of them, triumphing over them in it.

Rome thought it was the ultimate power in the world. The Romans controlled roads, seas, knowledge, and civilization itself. To maintain control, Rome used the standard tools of an empire: violence, oppression, and force. Every time Roman legions marched across the land, every time a Roman coin was used to buy or sell, every time a criminal was hoisted on a cross, it sent a single message: Rome is in control.

Yet, on that Friday in Jerusalem, Rome wasn't in control. They thought Jesus' crucifixion was another symbol of their power, but it wasn't. It was the climax of a story that had been written long before Rome ever existed and would continue long after Rome was gone. On the cross, and through the empty tomb, Jesus rendered them all powerless—Rome, Pilate, Caiaphas, sin, and even death itself. The resurrection is the ultimate declaration that God is in control.

5. Why do you think the government and religious leaders considered Jesus a threat? What did Jesus' ministry and teaching say about who was really in control of the world?

6. Who do you consider to be "in charge" in the world? How does Jesus' death and resurrection change the way you think about that person or group?

7. How did Jesus' death and resurrection disarm and triumph over the powers of Rome? How does it triumph over "the powers" in our lives today?

EXPERIENCING THE STORY

Think about your life. Where does Jesus threaten your control? In which parts of your life do you think you're in charge (family, finances, career, etc.)? What would it look like for Jesus to take control in those areas of your life? How will you give Him control?

EPISODE 7

MARY MAGDALENE

Lesson 1: Freedom

Lesson 2: Love

Lesson 3: Loss

Lesson 1
FREEDOM

Jesus saved Mary Magdalene from herself.
Who was she without Him?
— Jesus: His Life

Everything was new again. For the first time in a long time, Mary Magdalene felt alive. It was like the first day of spring after a long winter. Where everything once seemed cold and gray, now there was light, growth, and *life*!

It was all because of Jesus. She still couldn't believe it. For years she had heard them—those voices—otherworldly, obscene, oppressive. They covered her thoughts like fog. No matter what she did, she couldn't escape them. There was nowhere she could run, nowhere she could hide. No matter what she did, they always came back. They were always there, lurking in the dark corners of her mind.

Then He came. Everything inside of her wanted to run from Him, claw at Him—escape! It burned even to be near Him. Yet something deep inside her—deeper even than the voices—told her to stay.

Then He spoke. In an instant, the voices were silenced. The fog was lifted. The weight was gone. For the first time in as long as she could remember, she was free, at peace.

How could she not follow Him?

OPENING QUESTION

1. What is the best thing you've ever received for free? In what ways is faith a "free" gift?

READING THE STORY

Luke 8:1–3 (NKJV)

Now it came to pass, afterward, that He went through every city and village, preaching and bringing the glad tidings of the kingdom of God. And the twelve were with Him, and certain women who had been healed of evil spirits and infirmities—Mary called Magdalene, out of whom had come seven demons, and Joanna the wife of Chuza, Herod's steward, and Susanna, and many others who provided for Him from their substance.

Jesus became Mary Magdalene's teacher, and everything seemed possible.

— Jesus: His Life

ENGAGING THE STORY

2. If you had lived in the first century and had heard that someone in your town was healing sick people and preaching, what might be your first response?

3. Why do you think Mary Magdalene was so willing to travel with and financially support Jesus?

4. Some of Jesus' closest companions were fishermen, tax collectors, and women who were formerly possessed. What do you think this suggests about who Jesus was and what He valued?

EXPLORING THE THEMES

Luke 4:16–19 (NIV)

> *He went to Nazareth, where he had been brought up, and on the Sabbath day he went into the synagogue, as was his custom. He stood up to read, and the scroll of the prophet Isaiah was handed to him. Unrolling it, he found the place where it is written: "The Spirit of the Lord is on me, because he has anointed me to proclaim good news to the poor. He has sent me to proclaim freedom for the prisoners and recovery of sight for the blind, to set the oppressed free, to proclaim the year of the Lord's favor."*

John 8:33–36 (NIV)

> *They answered him, "We are Abraham's descendants and have never been slaves of anyone. How can you say that we shall be set free?" Jesus replied, "Very truly I tell you, everyone who sins is a slave to sin. Now a slave has no permanent place in the family, but a son belongs to it forever. So if the Son sets you free, you will be free indeed."*

Jesus had transformed Mary's life. Thanks to Him, she was free! The demons that had tormented her were gone, and now she could live according to God's design—a thriving, abundant life!

That's what Jesus offers to us today. He sets us free—free from past failures, sins, and even demons. When we encounter that kind of freedom, it's enticing. Just like Mary, it drives us to learn more about the person who brought us such an incredible gift, who changed and transformed our lives. When we find freedom through Jesus, we can't help but follow Him.

5. How does our culture define freedom? How is it similar to or different from the picture of freedom Jesus emphasized in His life and ministry?

6. What kinds of things hold people captive today? What might it look like for captive people to experience freedom through Jesus?

7. How does the freedom Jesus brings us change our relationship with God? How does it change our relationship with other people?

"So if the Son sets you free, you will be free indeed."

—John 8:36 (NIV)

EXPERIENCING THE STORY

How has God brought freedom in your life? How did it change your life? Who do you know who needs to hear about the freedom you experienced? What would it take for you to share the freedom Jesus gave you with the people you know and love?

Lesson 2
LOVE

"This is my commandment, that you love one another as I have loved you."
— John 15:12 (ESV)

It was too much to bear. She could see the way the crowd looked at Him with hate shining in their eyes. The priests had whipped the crowd into a frenzy—she could feel their energy and their hunger for violence and blood as they shouted insults at Him. The soldiers who stood beneath Him fed off the crowd. She could see their contempt as they divided up His clothing while they waited for Him to die.

The wind forced her to huddle closer to Mary as the sky darkened. It was just the two of them and John. Everyone else had fled, abandoning Him to the mockery of the crowds. She wished she had joined them; she wished she could scream, close her eyes, and stop the world. She wanted to let grief and pain wash her away.

But she couldn't. She wouldn't. She would watch, she would see, she would stay. As heartbreaking as it was to see Him hanging there, bleeding, screaming, and fighting for every breath, she would stay. They hung that sign above Him as their final humiliation, but she refused to let them mock what she knew was true. He *was* her King.

So she would stay with her King to the end.

OPENING QUESTION

1. What's a memorable way that your friends and family members have shown their love for you?

READING THE STORY

Matthew 27:45–56 (ESV)

Now from the sixth hour there was darkness over all the land until the ninth hour. And about the ninth hour Jesus cried out with a loud voice, saying, "Eli, Eli, lema sabachthani?" that is, "My God, my God, why have you forsaken me?" And some of the bystanders, hearing it, said, "This man is calling Elijah." And one of them at once ran and took a sponge, filled it with sour wine, and put it on a reed and gave it to him to drink. But the others said, "Wait, let us see whether Elijah will come to save him." And Jesus cried out again with a loud voice and yielded up his spirit. And behold, the curtain of the temple was torn in two, from top to bottom. And the earth shook, and the rocks were split. The tombs also were opened. And many bodies of the saints who had fallen asleep were raised, and coming out of the tombs after his resurrection they went into the holy city and appeared to many. When the centurion and those who were with him, keeping watch over Jesus, saw the earthquake and what took place, they were filled with awe and said, "Truly this was the Son of God!" There were also many women there, looking on from a distance, who had followed Jesus from Galilee, ministering to him, among whom were Mary Magdalene and Mary the mother of James and Joseph and the mother of the sons of Zebedee.

ENGAGING THE STORY

2. If you had been Mary, describe your feelings as you watched Jesus—the man who had changed your life—being humiliated and tortured by the Roman Empire.

3. Why do you think Mary stayed with Jesus during His crucifixion when most of His other followers ran away?

4. How do you think Jesus felt when He saw that several women, many of whom were His close friends, stayed nearby while He was being crucified?

Mary Magdalene could not be His warrior,
but she could be His witness.
—Jesus: His Life

EXPLORING THE THEMES

John 15:12–17 (ESV)

"This is my commandment, that you love one another as I have loved you. Greater love has no one than this, that someone lay down his life for his friends. You are my friends if you do what I command you. No longer do I call you servants, for the servant does not know what his master is doing; but I have called you friends, for all that I have heard from my Father I have made known to you. You did not choose me, but I chose you and appointed you that you should go and bear fruit and that your fruit should abide, so that whatever you ask the Father in my name, he may give it to you. These things I command you, so that you will love one another.

Isaiah 53:1–7 (ESV)

Who has believed what he has heard from us? And to whom has the arm of the Lord been revealed? For he grew up before him like a young plant, and like a root out of dry ground; he had no form or majesty that we should look at him, and no beauty that we should desire him. He was despised and rejected by men, a man of sorrows and acquainted with grief; and as one from whom men hide their faces he was despised, and we esteemed him not. Surely he has borne our griefs and carried our sorrows; yet we esteemed him stricken, smitten by God, and afflicted. But he was pierced for our transgressions; he was crushed for our iniquities; upon him was the chastisement that brought us peace, and with his wounds we are healed. All we like sheep have gone astray; we have turned—every one—to his own way; and the Lord has laid on him the iniquity of us all. He was oppressed, and he was afflicted, yet he opened not his mouth; like a lamb that is led to the slaughter, and like a sheep that before its shearers is silent, so he opened not his mouth.

Jesus' followers—including Mary and several others—imitated the love He showed them. The devotion and care they demonstrated for Him at the cross and in His burial were in response to the love He had shown them.

The cross is the ultimate symbol of God's love. It's where the Creator of the universe rescued humanity from the power of sin, death, and evil. These things entered the world through our actions. At the cross, however, God endured the suffering and pain we deserved, opening the door for us to live the way He originally created us to live.

5. Why do you think God chose to rescue humanity from the power of sin, death, and evil? Why didn't He let us endure the consequences of our choice to reject His authority?

6. How does our culture view and define love? How is the love God showed at the cross different from our culture's view of love?

7. How easy is it for you to believe that God died for you? How do you feel when you think about His sacrificial death on your behalf?

EXPERIENCING THE STORY

How have you experienced God's love? What would it look like for you to share His love with other people? How might that change their relationship with you?

Lesson 3

LOSS

Jesus' pain was over, but the confusion had just begun.

— Jesus: His Life

Any other time, she would have loved this place. The garden was peaceful and calm. He would have loved it here too. Now the peace and tranquility of the garden only magnified the chaos and grief in her soul. Jesus said He was the Messiah, yet the stone they rolled in front of His tomb said otherwise.

Someone had moved the stone for her. The realization cut through her grief. The stone. *Someone had moved the stone*! Panicked, she looked inside the tomb. Hot tears welled up as her fears were confirmed. It wasn't enough to kill Him; they had taken His body too.

They had taken Him away, and she couldn't find Him. One final insult for the man who had changed her life. One final cruelty—denying her the chance to anoint His body and give Him a decent burial. Through her tears, she saw a figure approach. Probably the gardener.

He might know what had happened to Jesus.

OPENING QUESTION

1. Have you ever lost an item that was important to you? Describe your thoughts, feelings, and actions after that time.

READING THE STORY

Luke 23:50–56 (NKJV)

Now behold, there was a man named Joseph, a council member, a good and just man. He had not consented to their decision and deed. He was from Arimathea, a city of the Jews, who himself was also waiting for the kingdom of God. This man went to Pilate and asked for the body of Jesus. Then he took it down, wrapped it in linen, and laid it in a tomb that was hewn out of the rock, where no one had ever lain before. That day was the Preparation, and the Sabbath drew near. And the women who had come with Him from Galilee followed after, and they observed the tomb and how His body was laid. Then they returned and prepared spices and fragrant oils. And they rested on the Sabbath according to the commandment.

ENGAGING THE STORY

2. What do you think Mary felt as she watched Joseph bury Jesus?

3. Mary and the disciples had spent three years following Jesus. If you had been one of the disciples, how might you have felt about those three years after you realized Jesus was dead?

4. How do you think Mary and the disciples felt on the Sabbath morning after Jesus had been buried? What do you think the day might have been like for them?

Mary Magdalene was lost, and Jesus found her.
She saw the resurrected Lord!
— Jesus: His Life

EXPLORING THE THEMES

John 20:1–3 (NKJV)

Now the first day of the week Mary Magdalene went to the tomb early, while it was still dark, and saw that the stone had been taken away from the tomb. Then she ran and came to Simon Peter, and to the other disciple, whom Jesus loved, and said to them, "They have taken away the Lord out of the tomb, and we do not know where they have laid Him." Peter therefore went out, and the other disciple, and were going to the tomb.

John 20:11–18 (NKJV)

But Mary stood outside by the tomb weeping, and as she wept she stooped down and looked into the tomb. And she saw two angels in white sitting, one at the head and the other at the feet, where the body of Jesus had lain. Then they said to her, "Woman, why are you weeping?" She said to them, "Because they have taken away my Lord, and I do not know where they have laid Him." Now when she had said this, she turned around and saw Jesus standing there, and did not know that it was Jesus. Jesus said to her, "Woman, why are you weeping? Whom are you seeking?" She, supposing Him to be the gardener, said to Him, "Sir, if You have carried Him away, tell me where You have laid Him, and I will take Him away." Jesus said to her, "Mary!" She turned and said to Him, "Rabboni!" (which is to say, Teacher). Jesus said to her, "Do not cling to Me, for I have not yet ascended to My Father; but go to My brethren and say to them, 'I am ascending to My Father and your Father, and to My God and your God.'" Mary Magdalene came and told the disciples that she had seen the Lord, and that He had spoken these things to her.

Jesus was alive! In an instant, the pain and grief Mary had battled for days were replaced with joy. This was inconceivable, unthinkable, unimaginable! Dead people didn't come back to life, yet here Jesus was, right in front of her!

Jesus' resurrection is the event that changed the world. Death had been defeated! The pain, loss, and suffering that humanity had always experienced no longer had the final word. Now there was a new body and new life not only for Jesus but also for His followers.

5. Describe how Mary might have felt when she saw Jesus for the first time after His resurrection. What might she have thought His resurrection meant for her and the other disciples?

6. How do many people deal with the loss of a loved one? How does Jesus' resurrection change the way we should view death?

7. How do you think Mary felt when Jesus said He would be ascending to His Father? How might her feelings have been different from what she experienced just after Jesus died?

EXPERIENCING THE STORY

Jesus' resurrection is proof that the power of sin, death, and evil has been defeated. How has Jesus defeated the power of sin and evil in your life? What might it look like for Him to defeat the power of sin and evil in the lives of people you know and love?

EPISODE 8

PETER

Lesson 1: Loyalty

Lesson 2: Disappointment

Lesson 3: Restoration

Lesson 1

LOYALTY

There was much Peter didn't understand about Jesus,
but he knew beyond the shadow of a doubt,
he would always be Jesus' devoted follower.
— Jesus: His Life

If anyone was going to change the world, it wasn't going to be Peter. He was a fisherman—blue collar and hard working. He probably couldn't read and most of his education had been practical: where to find fish, how to sail, how to fix his equipment. He was destined for a life of obscurity in Northern Israel, another anonymous laborer who would die and be forgotten.

When Jesus arrived, however, Peter's destiny changed in an instant. The moment Peter put aside his nets, he took his first step into a grander universe—into God's plan. Jesus offered Peter a chance to become part of a movement that would change the world. Instead of catching fish, Peter would become a fisher of men—someone who invited other people to have their lives changed by Jesus, just like his had been.

Peter embraced Jesus wholeheartedly. He became Jesus' right-hand man, His trusted and loyal companion. This was no surprise to Peter. After all, Jesus had changed Peter's life and given him a calling and a sense of significance. No matter where Jesus went, no matter what He did, Peter wanted to be there too.

OPENING QUESTION

1. Has there ever been an instance where a company or organization impressed you with their customer service? What happened? How did this experience increase your loyalty to the company?

READING THE STORY

Luke 5:1–11 (NIV)

One day as Jesus was standing by the Lake of Gennesaret, the people were crowding around him and listening to the word of God. He saw at the water's edge two boats, left there by the fishermen, who were washing their nets. He got into one of the boats, the one belonging to Simon, and asked him to put out a little from shore. Then he sat down and taught the people from the boat. When he had finished speaking, he said to Simon, "Put out into deep water, and let down the nets for a catch." Simon answered, "Master, we've worked hard all night and haven't caught anything. But because you say so, I will let down the nets." When they had done so, they caught such a large number of fish that their nets began to break. So they signaled their partners in the other boat to come and help them, and they came and filled both boats so full that they began to sink. When Simon Peter saw this, he fell at Jesus' knees and said, "Go away from me, Lord; I am a sinful man!" For he and all his companions were astonished at the catch of fish they had taken, and so were James and John, the sons of Zebedee, Simon's partners. Then Jesus said to Simon, "Don't be afraid; from now on you will fish for people." So they pulled their boats up on shore, left everything and followed him.

ENGAGING THE STORY

2. If you had been Peter, would you have immediately left everything you'd ever known to follow Jesus? Why or why not?

3. Why do you think Peter told Jesus to go away from him after the miraculous catch of fish?

4. What do you think Peter realized about Jesus at that moment? How might that have impacted the decisions Peter made? How do you think that impacted his relationship with Jesus?

"Then Jesus said to Simon [Peter], 'Don't be afraid; from now on you will fish for people.' So they pulled their boats up on shore, left everything and followed him."

— Luke 5:10b–11 (NIV)

EXPLORING THE THEMES

Matthew 16:13–18 (ESV)

Now when Jesus came into the district of Caesarea Philippi, he asked his disciples, "Who do people say that the Son of Man is?" And they said, "Some say John the Baptist, others say Elijah, and others Jeremiah or one of the prophets." He said to them, "But who do you say that I am?" Simon Peter replied, "You are the Christ, the Son of the living God." And Jesus answered him, "Blessed are you, Simon Bar-Jonah! For flesh and blood has not revealed this to you, but my Father who is in heaven. And I tell you, you are Peter, and on this rock I will build my church, and the gates of hell shall not prevail against it.

Matthew 16:21–23 (ESV)

From that time Jesus began to show his disciples that he must go to Jerusalem and suffer many things from the elders and chief priests and scribes, and be killed, and on the third day be raised. And Peter took him aside and began to rebuke him, saying, "Far be it from you, Lord! This shall never happen to you." But he turned and said to Peter, "Get behind me, Satan! You are a hindrance to me. For you are not setting your mind on the things of God, but on the things of man."

A 2017 CNN article reported that when Steve Jobs (former CEO and co-founder of Apple) tried to recruit a Pepsi Cola executive to work at Apple, he asked this question: "Do you want to sell sugar water for the rest of your life, or do you want to come with me and change the world?"

That's the same type of offer Jesus made to Peter—an opportunity to leave his old life behind and to do something that mattered, to be part of something bigger than himself. Peter's experiences with Jesus were what made him loyal to Jesus. That's why in one breath Peter could acknowledge Jesus as God's Son, and in the next, would refuse to let Jesus die.

Jesus makes this same offer to us that He made to Peter. When we choose to follow Him, we get to be part of His plan to change the world!

5. Think about your life. What organizations and people are you loyal to? Why?

6. How do you see Jesus using His followers to change the world today?

7. Think about your story. What has Jesus done in your life that makes you want to follow Him?

When Peter left all that behind, he felt like his life was just beginning.

— Jesus: His Life

EXPERIENCING THE STORY

Loyalty involves a commitment and a cost. For instance, when you are loyal to a certain team, you don't support an opposing team. What commitment have you made to Jesus? What has that commitment cost you? What has been the result of your commitment—how has it been worth the cost?

Lesson 2

DISAPPOINTMENT

Peter had no doubt in his mind that he would never deny Jesus.
He would defend Jesus to his death!

— Jesus: His Life

It had been the biggest and most tumultuous week of Peter's life. As Jesus entered Jerusalem to celebrate Passover, crowds of pilgrims traveling to the city had given Him a king's welcome. On top of that, Jesus had publicly and violently confronted the corruption of the religious leaders at the Temple. It was the start of everything Jesus' disciples had been waiting for—the fulfillment of a divine destiny, the start of a glorious new kingdom! The Messiah had come to God's holy city to save and to lead His people, and Peter was right beside Him.

Exciting as they had been, the events left Peter exhausted. As he gathered with Jesus to celebrate the Passover meal, he hoped this brief moment of peace would give him the strength he needed to continue to stand by Jesus in the days ahead. More than ever before, he would need to stay strong and confident. The High Priest was probably going to try to make trouble for Jesus, but Peter was committed. Nothing would separate him from Jesus. No matter what happened, he would defend his teacher, his friend, his king.

After all, Jesus was counting on him.

OPENING QUESTION

1. When was the last time you eagerly anticipated or were excited about an event or experience? When it finally happened, how did the actual experience measure up to your expectations?

____

____

____

____

____

____

READING THE STORY

Mark 14:27–31 (NIV)

"You will all fall away," Jesus told them, "for it is written: "'I will strike the shepherd, and the sheep will be scattered.' But after I have risen, I will go ahead of you into Galilee." Peter declared, "Even if all fall away, I will not." "Truly I tell you," Jesus answered, "today—yes, tonight—before the rooster crows twice you yourself will disown me three times." But Peter insisted emphatically, "Even if I have to die with you, I will never disown you." And all the others said the same.

Was Peter no better than Judas? Why did Peter deny Jesus? Fear? Cowardice? Everything Peter knew about himself was wrong.

— Jesus: His Life

ENGAGING THE STORY

2. Why do you think Peter and the other disciples were so confident they would never deny Jesus? How do you think Peter felt when Jesus said Peter would deny Him three times?

3. What are some of the most common areas of disappointment people experience? How do most people usually handle their disappointment?

4. What happens when someone allows failure and shame to define them? How do failure and shame impact a person's relationship with God? How do they impact the person's relationship with others?

EXPLORING THE THEMES

Mark 14:32–38 (NIV)

They went to a place called Gethsemane, and Jesus said to his disciples, "Sit here while I pray." He took Peter, James and John along with him, and he began to be deeply distressed and troubled. "My soul is overwhelmed with sorrow to the point of death," he said to them. "Stay here and keep watch." Going a little farther, he fell to the ground and prayed that if possible the hour might pass from him. "Abba, Father," he said, "everything is possible for you. Take this cup from me. Yet not what I will, but what you will." Then he returned to his disciples and found them sleeping. "Simon," he said to Peter, "are you asleep? Couldn't you keep watch for one hour? Watch and pray so that you will not fall into temptation. The spirit is willing, but the flesh is weak."

Mark 14:66–72 (NIV)

While Peter was below in the courtyard, one of the servant girls of the high priest came by. When she saw Peter warming himself, she looked closely at him. "You also were with that Nazarene, Jesus," she said. But he denied it. "I don't know or understand what you're talking about," he said, and went out into the entryway. When the servant girl saw him there, she said again to those standing around, "This fellow is one of them." Again he denied it. After a little while, those standing near said to Peter, "Surely you are one of them, for you are a Galilean." He began to call down curses, and he swore to them, "I don't know this man you're talking about." Immediately the rooster crowed the second time. Then Peter remembered the word Jesus had spoken to him: "Before the rooster crows twice you will disown me three times." And he broke down and wept.

In one night, everything Peter believed about himself came crashing down. Hours after he had boldly proclaimed he would never deny the Lord, Peter had failed his friend and mentor twice. The first was in Gethsemane, in Jesus' moment of need, when Peter had fallen asleep. The second—a much worse failure—came when Peter denied that he ever knew Jesus. As morning came, shame overshadowed

Peter. He hadn't lived up to his expectations; he had disappointed and denied Jesus. How could he live with himself?

Fortunately the story didn't end there. Jesus didn't let Peter's shame define him or defeat him. Thankfully, Jesus does the same thing for us! We all have had times when we've disappointed God and other people. Because of those times we're tempted to let shame define us. The good news is that Jesus sets us free from our failure and shame so we can follow Him!

5. Why do you think Peter denied that he knew Jesus? Do you think his actions were justified? Why or why not?

6. What emotions do you think Peter experienced when he heard the rooster crow, and he realized he had broken the promise he made to Jesus?

7. Both Judas and Peter turned their backs on Jesus. What differences do you see between the stories of Peter and Judas?

EXPERIENCING THE STORY

When have you felt shame because you disappointed or failed God or other people? What would it look like for God to set you free from your shame? How would that freedom change your relationship with God? How would it change your relationship with other people?

Lesson 3

RESTORATION

Peter no longer felt ashamed. This was his chance to finally tell Jesus how sorry he was.

— Jesus: His Life

Jesus had come back to life! God had done the impossible—*He had raised Jesus from the dead!* Any doubt the disciples had about whether Jesus was the Messiah had been erased when they saw the risen Jesus. Everything He had said about Himself was true!

Peter wasn't as joyful as the rest of the disciples. Yes, Jesus had risen from the dead, but that meant Peter hadn't just denied and abandoned his friend and teacher, he had actually abandoned God's Son. When Jesus needed him most, Peter hadn't been there. He gave in to his fear. He fled for his own safety. He failed. Surely, there was no forgiveness for deserting the Messiah.

The man Jesus called the rock had proven himself to be as weak as sand when it really mattered. Was he any better than Judas, the one who had betrayed all of them? As the other disciples rejoiced and wondered what Jesus' resurrection meant for their future, Peter prepared to go back to his old life of fishing.

After all, why would Jesus give him another chance?

OPENING QUESTION

1. Have you ever tried to repair something instead of throwing it away? Why did you make that decision?

READING THE STORY

John 21:1–7 (NIV)

Afterward Jesus appeared again to his disciples, by the Sea of Galilee. It happened this way: Simon Peter, Thomas (also known as Didymus), Nathanael from Cana in Galilee, the sons of Zebedee, and two other disciples were together. "I'm going out to fish," Simon Peter told them, and they said, "We'll go with you." So they went out and got into the boat, but that night they caught nothing. Early in the morning, Jesus stood on the shore, but the disciples did not realize that it was Jesus. He called out to them, "Friends, haven't you any fish?" "No," they answered.

He said, "Throw your net on the right side of the boat and you will find some." When they did, they were unable to haul the net in because of the large number of fish. Then the disciple whom Jesus loved said to Peter, "It is the Lord!" As soon as Simon Peter heard him say, "It is the Lord," he wrapped his outer garment around him (for he had taken it off) and jumped into the water.

ENGAGING THE STORY

2. Why do you think Peter decided to go fishing? How do you think he felt as he climbed back into the boat?

3. If you had been Peter, how would you have felt when you saw Jesus standing on the shore? Why?

4. What similarities do you see between Peter's first encounter with Jesus (Luke 5:1–11) and this meeting? What do you think Jesus wanted to communicate to Peter through the similar experiences?

From that day on, Peter knew he would be able to do whatever Jesus commanded of him.

— Jesus: His Life

EXPLORING THE THEMES

John 21:15–19 (NIV)

When they had finished eating, Jesus said to Simon Peter, "Simon son of John, do you love me more than these?" "Yes, Lord," he said, "you know that I love you." Jesus said, "Feed my lambs." Again Jesus said, "Simon son of John, do you love me?" He answered, "Yes, Lord, you know that I love you." Jesus said, "Take care of my sheep." The third time he said to him, "Simon son of John, do you love me?" Peter was hurt because Jesus asked him the third time, "Do you love me?" He said, "Lord, you know all things; you know that I love you." Jesus said, "Feed my sheep. Very truly I tell you, when you were younger you dressed yourself and went where you wanted; but when you are old you will stretch out your hands, and someone else will dress you and lead you where you do not want to go." Jesus said this to indicate the kind of death by which Peter would glorify God. Then he said to him, "Follow me!"

Acts 2:1–4, 14a (NIV)

When the day of Pentecost came, they were all together in one place. Suddenly a sound like the blowing of a violent wind came from heaven and filled the whole house where they were sitting. They saw what seemed to be tongues of fire that separated and came to rest on each of them. All of them were filled with the Holy Spirit and began to speak in other tongues as the Spirit enabled them. . . . Then Peter stood up with the Eleven, raised his voice and addressed the crowd . . . .

Several days earlier, Peter had denied that he even knew Jesus. Now, as he sat face-to-face with the man he had failed, Peter probably expected Jesus to rebuke him or maybe even shame him for his failure. Instead, Jesus asked three times if Peter loved Him. Three denials, three questions, three affirmations. Jesus said nothing about the failure! Instead, Peter's failure was set aside for a greater calling.

Jesus didn't want Peter to live in shame. Rather, Jesus wanted Peter to step into leading and serving His church. A month later, that's exactly what Peter did. The next time Peter was asked about Jesus, he didn't hide or make denials; he boldly proclaimed who Jesus was and what He had done. That's what Jesus does for us! He calls us out of shame and failure—He redeems and restores us—so we can boldly and confidently tell other people about Him.

5. If you had been in Jesus' shoes, what would you have said to Peter? Why?

6. What impact do you think Jesus' forgiveness had on Peter? How do you think it changed the way Peter saw himself?

7. How should Peter's restoration change the way we view our own mistakes and failures?

EXPERIENCING THE STORY

Think about your life before you decided to follow Jesus (or think about a time you really failed Jesus). What was it like? Think about your life now. How has God restored you? How has that restoration impacted your life? Spend some time thanking Him for His goodness to you.

NOTES

NOTES

NOTES

NOTES

NOTES

NOTES

NOTES

NOTES